Policy Papers
in International Affairs

NUMBER 21

D1283443

WITHDRAWN

Emerging Japanese Economic Influence in Africa

IMPLICATIONS FOR THE UNITED STATES

Joanna Moss &
John Ravenhill

Institute of
International Studies

UNIVERSITY OF CALIFORNIA • BERKELEY

In sponsoring the Policy Papers in International Affairs series, the Institute of International Studies reasserts its commitment to a vigorous policy debate by providing a forum for innovative approaches to important policy issues. The views expressed in each paper are those of the author(s) only, and publication in this series does not constitute endorsement by the Institute.

HF
1602.15
.A4
M67
1985

International Standard Book Number 0-87725-521-0

Library of Congress Card Catalog Number 84-82151

© 1985 by the Regents of the University of California

CONTENTS

LIST OF TABLES

List of Tables

List of Tables

LIST OF FIGURES

ACKNOWLEDGMENTS

The authors wish to extend their thanks to Ravi Thomas for his tireless statistical analyses. Fitzgerald Sarramegna provided additional research assistance for Chapters 3 and 4. The American Embassy's staff in Tokyo was most helpful. Our special thanks go to staff members Mr. Takai and Douglas Dearborn for gathering information and helping set up interviews, and to Marc Bass for enriching this study with insightful comments on an earlier draft. Namiki Hideo is gratefully acknowledged for his Japanese literature search and translation. Thanks also to Rebecca Schulmann for her efforts in literature search and to Julie Layton for her assistance in word processing. Skillful editing by Bojana Ristich greatly improved the manuscript. Last but not least, the much appreciated word-processing, software development, and editorial efforts of Joanna's husband, Robert Sonderegger, were crucial to the successful completion of this study.

A first draft of this study was written for the U.S. Department of State, Office of External Research, under Contract No. 1722-220120. The authors bear sole responsibility for the contents of this study.

Chapter 1

INTRODUCTION

One of the major changes in policy toward the Third World introduced by the Reagan administration has been a new emphasis on the private sector. There are two thrusts to this policy: first, the encouragement of indigenous private enterprise in Third World countries, and second, the promotion of U.S. commercial interests there. For the latter to be successful, policymakers need to have detailed information regarding the performance of the U.S. private sector in comparison to its principal competitors. From such data it may be possible to deduce the reasons for differences in performance and especially to identify whether the competitors receive support from their governments which is not available to U.S. corporations.

Our principal goal in this study is to compare the performance of the U.S. private sector with that of Japan in one Third-World area —Africa.* In recent years concern in the United States regarding the Japanese economic challenge has reached a level similar to that expressed in Europe in the 1960s regarding *le défi américain*. Much has been written on the Japanese penetration of the American market, but relatively little attention has been given to a second dimension of U.S.-Japanese competition: the search for export markets and secure sources of supply of raw materials in the Third World. Developing countries now account for over 35 percent of U.S. exports and over 45 percent of U.S. imports (the equivalent figures for Japan are 45 and 60 percent respectively); thus this is a dangerous omission.[1] To lose the commercial battle with Japan in the Third World could

*For the purposes of this study "Africa" is defined as the countries of sub-Saharan Africa, including South Africa. In examining the evolution of commercial relations, we shall make use of a number of subgroupings (detailed in Chapter 2).

1

have serious long-term repercussions for the development of the U.S. economy.

We have chosen to focus on Africa since it represents a relatively "neutral" market for competition between U.S. and Japanese exporters. In large part, this is an exploratory study. There is very little written in either English or Japanese on relations between Japan and Africa; our search of the literature in both languages uncovered only one (not very satisfactory) work of monograph length.[2] Similarly, there is surprisingly little written on U.S. economic relations with Africa. Too often the African market has been perceived as a European preserve; this tendency is encouraged by the lack of information on African opportunities available to the U.S. private sector. To the best of our knowledge, ours is the first comprehensive study of Japanese economic relations with Africa, and at the same time it presents a detailed overview of recent U.S. economic relations with the continent.

At present Africa is of relatively minor significance as a trading partner or a host for investment for either the United States or Japan. In recent years the continent has accounted for less than 2.5 percent of U.S. export sales and 7 percent of total U.S. imports; it accounts for only 3 percent of U.S. overall direct investment worldwide. Similarly, trade with Africa amounts to barely 3.5 percent of the Japanese total, while investments in the region account for a mere 2 percent of overall Japanese foreign investment. However, to dwell on the magnitude of these figures would be an overly static approach. Africa is an increasingly important source of raw materials (especially petroleum and minerals) and an expanding market for capital and consumer goods. This competition between the United States and Japan in Africa is a microcosm of their global commercial rivalry.

Table 1-1 provides an indication of the significance of Africa as a supplier of raw materials for both countries. Considering Japan's overall dependence on imported raw materials, it is surprising that the United States overall is more dependent on Africa as a source of supply. In addition, in marked contrast to the United States, Japanese dependence is heavily concentrated (with the exceptions of copper and cobalt) on the Republic of South Africa. Black African sources of bauxite, chromium, cobalt, and manganese are a much higher percentage of total U.S. imports than of Japanese. Africa

Table 1-1

U.S. AND JAPANESE IMPORT RELIANCE FOR RAW MATERIALS, 1980
(*Percent*)

Raw Material	United States			Japan		
	Net World Import Reliance	African Share[a]	South African Share	Net World Import Reliance	African Share[a]	South African Share
Antimony ore	53%	20%	9%	N.A.	1%	1%
Asbestos	76	9	8	N.A.	37	20
Bauxite/ aluminum	94	6	0	100%	4	0
Chromium	91	39	34	N.A.	41	41
Coal	0	N.A.	N.A.	82	10	10
Cobalt	91	55	0	N.A.	25	0
Copper	18[b]	6[c]	6[b]	96	18	2
Ferro chromium	91	75	68	N.A.	78	N.A.
Fluorspar	84	28	27	N.A.	27	25
Iron ore	28[b]	4	0	99	6	5
Lead	30[b]	16	16	84	10	8
Manganese ore	97	54	24	92[c]	56	49
Tin ore	77[b]	14	14	98	0	0
Titanium ore	N.A.	29	10	N.A.	56	56
Zirconium	N.A.	15	15		19	19

Source: For United States—U.S. Bureau of the Census, *U.S. Imports*; for Japan— Japan External Trade Organization (JETRO): *White Paper on International Trade 1982* (Tokyo), and *Japan Exports and Imports* (Tokyo, 1981).

[a]Includes South Africa.

[b]Data for 1973.

[c]Data for 1975.

also contributes 20 percent of the total U.S. imports of oil; the figure for Japan is only 2.5 percent.

While Africa is a relatively minor economic partner for both the United States and Japan, it is certainly not one that can or should be ignored. For our purposes the African market provides a unique location for comparing the success of U.S. and Japanese business in expanding trade in recent years. African countries, unlike those of Latin America or Southeast Asia, are not "natural" economic allies— or, more pointedly, satellites—of either the United States or Japan. Both countries are geographically removed from the African continent and consequently face greater transportation costs than (say) European countries. Neither country had strong economic ties with the continent prior to the independence of the majority of Black African countries in the late 1950s and early 1960s. In most cases both were at a disadvantage compared to the close relations enjoyed by the European powers with their former colonies. Neither country had a colonial history in Africa. Although the United States had long-standing ties with Liberia, Japan had its most developed economic relations with that country as a result of the use by Japanese shipping companies of the Liberian flag of convenience. Japanese corporations were of course at a disadvantage compared to their American equivalents in dealing with Anglophone Africa; both faced language barriers in Francophone and Lusophone (Portuguese-speaking) Africa.* Furthermore, on receiving independence, many African countries followed the decision of their former colonial metropoles, the United Kingdom and France, to deny most-favored-nation status to Japan, taking advantage of Article XXXV of the General Agreement on Tariffs and Trade (GATT).

At the beginning of the 1960s both the United States and Japan had a relatively good diplomatic standing in Africa. U.S. support in multinational forums for national self-determination, the education of many members of the post-independence ruling African elites in American universities, links between the Black community in the United States and in African countries, and the enthusiasm for Third

---

*Though the United States might appear to have an advantage in English-speaking Africa, the Japanese should not be any more handicapped than they usually are in non-Asian markets since they must speak English by necessity in most of their international transactions.

4

World "development," which was very pronounced during the Kennedy Administration and was reflected in substantial U.S. aid to the continent—all contributed to the positive image held by many African leaders of the United States. Japan's high diplomatic stature was for somewhat different reasons: its formidable record of economic achievement and its membership in the Afro-Asian Solidarity Organization led many Africans to view it as a successful non-Western model for development. Japan's lack of familiarity with Africa, however, might be considered a disadvantage: it was not until 1961 that an Africa Department was created in the Japanese Foreign Office.

In subsequent years the U.S. image in Africa became somewhat tarnished. The war in Vietnam, U.S. supplies of military equipment to its NATO ally Portugal (despite African protests that these were aiding the Portuguese in their struggle against African nationalist movements), the lack of effective pressure against the white minority regimes of the southern part of the continent, domestic racial problems, and African perceptions of U.S. intransigence in the North-South dialogue—all at times caused anger among African leaders. Meanwhile, Japan was not immune to criticism: the paucity of its aid effort, its breaking of sanctions during the Unilateral Declaration of Independence (UDI) period in Rhodesia (1965-80), its investments in mining and construction activities in the Portuguese colonies, its continued high volumes of trade and investment with South Africa and Namibia, the "honorary white" status conferred on Japanese visitors by South Africa in 1961, and its unwillingness to go beyond nominal support for the Group of 77 in the North-South dialogue—all aroused African anger.

Yet African criticism of Japan did not reach the same intensity as that leveled at the United States. On a variety of issues Japan has been able to shelter behind the hard-line stance taken by the United States. (For example, it could abstain on UN votes on North-South issues secure in the knowledge that the United States would cast a veto.)[3] Japan has been most successful in pursuing the principle of *seikei bunri*, the separation of economics from politics. By virtue of its superpower role, the United States has not had the same freedom to fudge issues: its policies inevitably have been more visible, thereby rendering the country more vulnerable to African criticism.

An examination of data on aggregate trade between Africa and the two countries tends to confirm initial impressions that Japan has been markedly more successful in recent years than the United States in penetrating the expanding African market. Whereas in the period 1960-70 U.S. and Japanese exports to Africa grew at approximately the same average annual rate (the Japanese from a lower absolute base, making the U.S. performance more impressive), from 1970-80 Japan's exports were expanding at a rate more than 50 percent above that of U.S. exports. Whereas Japanese exports to Africa were only 55.5 percent of the value of U.S. exports in 1960 and 57.1 percent in 1970, by 1980 they had reached 82.8 percent. By 1980 Japan had almost equaled the value of U.S. exports to Black Africa (see Table 1-2).

Between 1960 and 1980 U.S. imports from Africa grew at a much higher rate than Japanese imports. One result of these differential rates of increase was a marked turnaround in the balance of trade between the two countries and Africa. In 1960 and 1970 the United States enjoyed a small surplus on its African trade. Although in 1960 Japanese exports were worth more than three times its imports, by 1970 trade was approximately in balance. However, by 1980 the United States was running a huge trade deficit with the continent— nearly double the U.S. deficit on bilateral trade with Japan and equivalent to over 50 percent of the worldwide deficit in that year.[4] In the same year Japanese exports to Africa exceeded imports by a ratio of 7 to 4.

Only the strictest of mercantilist approaches would suggest that there is a need to balance trade by continental trading partner. There may indeed be sound economic reasons why it is in the U.S. interest to run a trade deficit with Africa. Nor are we suggesting that the United States and Japan have identical interests in their commercial relations with the Third World in general or Africa in particular. For the Japanese, foreign trade is not an optional matter; it is an economic necessity. Being an island country nearly devoid of natural resources, Japan depends heavily on foreign exchange to supply the minerals, fuels, and agricultural products it lacks. More than 70 percent of Japanese imports are food and raw materials. Nearly a third of total Japanese GNP is devoted to export and import activities. These very serious economic constraints have molded the course of Japanese economic evolution.

Viewing Japan historically also helps to understand the country's

Table 1-2

AFRICA'S TRADE WITH THE UNITED STATES AND JAPAN, 1960-80
(Millions of dollars)

	African Exports			African Imports		
	1960	1970	1980	1960	1970	1980
Africa						
United States	$530	$909	$16206	$604	$1273	$5770
Japan	108	711	2718	335	727	4775
Black Africa						
United States	447	728	14081	310	680	3106
Japan	66	458	1167	272	417	3243
Africa excluding Nigeria						
United States	486	767	5735	597	1119	4505
Japan	76	702	2608	257	660	3124

Sources: International Monetary Fund (IMF), *Direction of Trade Statistics Yearbook*, 1970-81.

drive for foreign markets. With the Meiji restoration in the 1860s, Japan ended its economic and political isolation and began the process of rapid economic development and industrialization. The economic constraints resulting from the limited resource base were dealt with by concentrating on export trade and duplicating industrial processes existent in the West. As labor productivity rose and rapid capital accumulation took place, Japan developed a comparative advantage in manufacturing. Although this process was interrupted by World War II, speedy Japanese postwar reconstruction ensured its continuation. Japan's participation in international trade reflects an interplay between two basic characteristics: Japan's need to import natural resources and its ability to export the product of highly skilled, capital-assisted human resources.

In contrast, the United States, with its huge domestic market and more abundant domestic supply of raw materials, has not had the same structural need for foreign trade. But with an increased dependence on foreign oil and the American taste for imports, foreign trade and foreign markets have grown in importance. No country can afford to do substantially worse in its commerce with third parties than a major competitor with similar trading interests. The figures on the development of U.S. and Japanese trade with Africa present a prima facie reason for concern.

The objective of this study is to examine in detail the commercial relations between the United States and Africa and Japan and Africa in order to ascertain in which areas (if any) the performance of the United States has lagged behind that of Japan and to explore the policy implications of these developments.

Chapter 2

TRADE RELATIONS BETWEEN
THE UNITED STATES AND AFRICA
AND JAPAN AND AFRICA

As we have noted, Africa is not a major commercial partner for the United States or Japan, either in terms of total trade or their trade with the developing world (less developed countries--LDCs). The importance of African trade in total U.S. exports has remained virtually unchanged over the 1970s, but Africa's share in total U.S. imports has more than doubled, to nearly 7 percent. Most of this increase is accounted for by oil imports from Nigeria. Africa's share in U.S. imports from non-oil-exporting LDCs has increased slightly over the last decade, in contrast to its share in Japanese imports. On the other hand, Africa's share in U.S. exports to LDCs has fallen slightly, but in contrast to the Japanese pattern, Africa's share in U.S. imports from LDCs has increased (Table 2-1).

There is a marked contrast in the recent history of Japanese commerce with Africa. The continent accounts for less than 4 percent of total Japanese trade and only 7.4 percent of Japanese exports to and 3.8 percent of Japanese imports from LDCs respectively. Even when petroleum is excluded, non-oil-exporting Africa comprises less than 10 percent of the Japanese export-import trade with non-oil producing LDCs. Over the last decade Africa's share in total Japanese imports has fallen by 50 percent. Its share in Japanese exports has not changed significantly; however, even if oil imports are excluded, Africa's share in Japanese imports has fallen dramatically (Table 2-2).

As Tables 2-1—2-6 show, two countries—Nigeria and South Africa—figure prominently in both U.S. and Japanese commercial relations with Africa. Oil imports from Nigeria account for over half of all U.S. imports from the continent. Purchases of Nigerian oil

9

Table 2-1

AFRICA'S SHARE IN U.S. TRADE, 1970-81

(Percent)

	1970	1971	1972	1973	1974	1975	1976	1977	1978	1979	1980	1981
U.S. Imports												
African share in total imports	2.6%	2.5%	2.4%	3.0%	5.4%	6.1%	6.8%	6.9%	5.6%	6.7%	7.5%	6.2%
African share in imports from LDCs	9.5	9.6	9.1	10.1	13.5	15.0	15.8	15.2	13.8	15.1	16.1	14.3
of which:												
Nigerian share	6.9	11.5	20.4	31.4	60.8	56.0	62.4	62.0	50.3	59.7	59.6	56.3
South African share	28.3	25.3	24.4	18.2	11.3	13.5	10.8	12.1	22.3	18.2	17.7	15.0
African (excluding Nigerian) share in imports from non-oil-exporting LDCs	10.4	10.1	8.7	8.8	8.5	12.1	12.0	12.0	12.7	11.6	12.4	10.9
U.S. Exports												
African share in total exports	2.7	3.0	2.4	2.2	2.5	2.8	2.8	2.6	2.3	1.9	2.5	2.8
African share in exports to LDCs	8.6	9.3	10.6	7.4	7.2	7.8	7.9	7.4	6.4	5.5	6.6	7.2
of which:												
Nigerian share	11.1	13.0	9.8	10.0	11.6	17.6	24.1	30.4	29.1	18.3	21.1	23.1
South African share	47.9	47.3	51.3	46.6	47.9	42.8	42.3	33.5	32.0	41.3	45.1	44.2

Source: International Monetary Fund (IMF), *Direction of Trade Statistics Yearbook, 1970-1981.*

Table 2-2

AFRICA'S SHARE IN JAPAN'S TRADE, 1970-81
(Percent)

	1970	1971	1972	1973	1974	1975	1976	1977	1978	1979	1980	1981
Japan's Imports												
African share in total imports	5.4%	4.7%	4.7%	4.3%	3.7%	3.4%	2.7%	2.6%	2.6%	2.6%	2.4%	2.4%
African share in imports from LDCs	13.3	10.6	10.9	9.9	6.9	6.0	4.8	4.6	4.7	4.5	3.9	3.9
of which:												
Nigerian share	1.3	2.9	7.2	11.6	19.4	14.4	6.2	1.1	0.4	1.5	3.5	10.0
South African share	33.4	36.2	36.7	32.0	33.6	45.3	43.6	48.3	52.0	46.3	52.2	51.5
African (excluding Nigerian) share in imports from non-oil-exporting LDCs	21.0	18.3	18.6	15.3	14.2	13.6	11.5	11.5	11.1	10.8	10.9	9.7
Japan's Exports												
African share in total imports	3.9	3.9	3.2	3.5	3.6	3.8	3.0	3.4	3.0	2.7	3.6	3.7
African share in exports to LDCs	10.1	10.4	8.9	8.9	8.6	8.3	7.3	7.8	6.8	6.0	7.9	8.3
of which:												
Nigerian share	8.4	10.3	13.7	10.8	14.1	27.4	28.5	36.6	32.1	29.5	32.2	38.0
South African share	44.0	44.2	39.7	45.6	47.7	40.9	35.2	27.5	33.1	36.4	38.8	39.1

Source: IMF, *Direction of Trade Statistics Yearbook, 1970-81.*

Table 2-3

U.S. EXPORTS TO MAJOR AFRICAN TRADING PARTNERS, 1981

Country	Export Volume (Millions of dollars)	Share of African Total (Percent)	Share of Black African Total (Percent)
South Africa	$2,912	44.5%	—
Nigeria	1,523	23.3	41.9%
Angola	268	4.1	7.4
Sudan	208	3.2	5.7
Ghana	154	2.3	4.2
Cameroon	152	2.3	4.2
Kenya	150	2.3	4.1
Zaire	141	2.2	3.9
Ivory Coast	130	1.9	3.6
Liberia	129	1.9	3.5
Gabon	128	1.9	3.5
Zambia	68	1.0	1.8
Ethiopia	62	0.9	1.7
Somalia	59	0.9	1.6
Guinea	53	0.8	1.5
Tanzania	48	0.7	1.3
Other	464	7.0	12.2
TOTAL	6,549	100.0	100.0

Source: IMF, *Direction of Trade Statistics Yearbook*, 1982.

account for a change in the balance between Nigeria and South Africa as principal continental sources of U.S. imports from Africa over the 1970-81 period. In the first three years of the 1970s Nigeria overtook South Africa as the principal source and now outsells South Africa in the U.S. market by a margin of almost 4:1. South Africa, on the other hand, remains the most important market for U.S. exports in subSaharan Africa. Nigeria's share of U.S. exports to the continent in 1981 had not risen to the peak reached in 1977, when its share was almost equal to that of South Africa.

South Africa and Nigeria are also key trading partners for Japan, but their roles in Japanese exports and imports are different from their respective contributions to U.S. trade. They account for

Table 2-4

U.S. IMPORTS FROM MAJOR AFRICAN TRADING PARTNERS, 1981

Country	Import Volume (Millions of dollars)	Share of African Total (Percent)	Share of Black African Total (Percent)
Nigeria	$9,554	56.2%	66.1%
South Africa	2,553	15.0	—
Angola	938	5.5	6.5
Cameroom	654	3.8	4.5
Gabon	455	2.7	3.1
Zaire	440	2.6	3.0
Ivory Coast	372	2.2	2.6
Congo	295	1.7	2.0
Ghana	255	1.5	1.6
Liberia	137	0.8	0.9
Botswana	135	0.8	0.9
Guinea	131	0.8	0.9
Zambia	118	0.7	0.8
Zimbabwe	116	0.7	0.8
Other	847	5.0	5.9
TOTAL	17,000	100.0	100.0

Source: Same as Table 2-3.

about the same percent of Japanese exports to Africa; together they account for over three fourths of Japanese sales in Africa. Between 1974 and 1976 Nigeria's share in Japan's exports to the continent more than doubled; in 1977 Japan sold more to Nigeria than to South Africa. By 1981 Japan's exports to Nigeria exceeded those of the United States. Although Japan trades with every country on the African continent, eleven account for 90 percent of Japanese exports, with Nigeria alone consuming more than 60 percent of Japanese sales to Black Africa (i.e., Africa excluding South Africa). U.S. exports to Africa are somewhat less concentrated than those of Japan.

As in the case of exports, 90 percent of Japanese imports from Africa come from eleven countries; over half originate in South Africa. In fact, since the 1970s the importance of South Africa as a

Table 2-5

JAPANESE EXPORTS TO MAJOR AFRICAN TRADING PARTNERS, 1981

Country	Export Volume (Millions of dollars)	Share of African Total (Percent)	Share of Black African Total (Percent)
South Africa	$2,222	39.1%	—
Nigeria	2,159	38.0	62.4%
Kenya	143	2.5	4.2
Sudan	101	1.8	2.9
Tanzania	93	1.6	2.7
Ivory Coast	87	1.5	2.5
Zaire	80	1.4	2.3
Ethiopia	66	1.2	1.9
Zambia	52	0.9	1.5
Liberia	46	0.8	1.3
Ghana	33	0.6	0.9
Other	596	10.3	17.7
TOTAL	5,678	100.0	100.0

Source: Same as Table 2-3.

source of imports has increased dramatically. Although the United States has a larger absolute total of imports from South Africa than does Japan, the South African share in total U.S. imports from the continent is much smaller. In contrast to its role in U.S. imports, Nigeria has a relatively minor share in total Japanese imports from sub-Saharan Africa, owing in part to the fact that Japanese companies have been reluctant to agree to the terms demanded by the Nigerian government for participation in oil production.

Below we shall first present a statistical market-share analysis of U.S. and Japanese trade with Africa in order to determine whether there have been statistically significant changes in the pattern of trade during the 1970s. Then we shall examine changes in the composition of trade between the parties.

Table 2-6

JAPANESE IMPORTS FROM MAJOR AFRICAN
TRADING PARTNERS, 1981

Country	Import Volume (Millions of dollars)	Share of African Total (Percent)	Share of Black African Total (Percent)
South Africa	$1,752	51.5%	—
Nigeria	339	10.0	20.6%
Liberia	308	9.1	18.7
Zambia	272	8.0	16.5
Ghana	119	3.5	7.2
Zaire	71	2.1	4.3
Sudan	57	1.7	3.4
Ivory Coast	51	1.5	3.1
Ethiopia	31	0.9	1.9
Mozambique	27	0.8	1.6
Tanzania	19	0.6	1.2
Other	354	10.4	21.5
TOTAL	3,400	100.0	100.0

Source: Same as Table 2-3.

MARKET-SHARE ANALYSIS

Recent changes in African trade arrangements with the European Community (EC) have offered freer access to African markets for non-EC industrial countries. Prior to independence the external trade of most African countries was dominated by the European colonial powers. Typically half to two thirds of a colony's trade was conducted with the metropole. After independence several preferential arrangements helped maintain this pattern. The former colonies kept their trade ties with the EC through the Yaoundé Conventions (1964-69, 1970-75), which provided a system of reciprocal trade preferences: the EC member-states were given tariff preferences in African markets in return for granting the Africans trade preferences in the EC over other Third World suppliers. The East African states of Kenya, Tanzania, and Uganda signed a special trade accord with the EC, the Arusha Agreement (1970-75), which provided mutual trade preferences for specified quantities of important export products. In addition, the Commonwealth Preferential Trading System among the Anglophone African states and members of the Commonwealth provided trade preferences for Commonwealth Africa in the United Kingdom market.

In 1975 agreements known as the Lomé Convention were reached between the former European colonies in Africa, the Caribbean, and the Pacific (ACP) and the EC, changing the preferential trading system markedly.*   The ACP countries were granted duty-free access to the EC for most of their exports (with the exception of products included in the EC's Common Agricultural Policy, where ACP production was in competition with that of European farmers). However, no reverse preferences were required for European goods in African markets.†   This was a break with the historic pattern of trade arrangements which had given the Europeans an institutionalized edge over other industrial suppliers such as the United States and Japan.   From the perspective of the latter, the Lomé Conventions provided easier access to African markets.   However, some African countries continue to favor the Europeans through licensing and quota arrangements.

The changes in Africa's commercial relations with the EC provided new trading possibilities in the second half of the 1970s for both American and Japanese exporters.   Accordingly, in our statistical analysis we shall examine trade during the 1970s, comparing the period 1970-75, when the Europeans had preferences in African markets, with the period 1976-81, when European advantages in the African market were reduced to non-tariff factors.

STATISTICAL ANALYSIS OF TRADE PATTERNS

In the 1970s considerable changes occurred in the trading patterns of industrialized countries with the developing world.   An oil price explosion and resultant world inflation greatly increased the

---

*The first Lomé Convention (Lomé I) was signed in February 1975; all of its trade provisions were operating by 1976.   Lomé I ran until 1979; its trade provisions are maintained by its successor, the Lomé II Convention, which is currently in force (1980-84).

†An exception to the non-reverse preference rule is Senegal, which continues to give preference to EC goods in its markets.

value of world trade as measured in current prices and changed long-established trading patterns. World trade grew at an average annual rate of 28.2 percent in the period 1970-73 and then at an annual rate of 31.3 percent until 1981. Whereas in 1970-73 the share of oil-exporting countries of world exports was 9 percent, it averaged 14 percent for 1974-81.

Any study of trade patterns of African countries during the 1970s will inevitably be biased by these structural changes in the world economy. As far as possible this study attempts to remove such biases. First, with a market-share approach, inflationary distortions in the data are neutralized. Second, by separating the oil-producing African and Third World countries from non-oil producers, we can isolate the effects of trade in petroleum.

In order to determine statistically significant changes in trading patterns between the United States, Japan, and Africa, export and import data are transformed into market shares for each year in 1970-81.* For example, in 1981 African exports to the world totaled $66.0 billion, of which $3.07 billion went to Japan; thus the Japanese share in African exports was 5 percent. Each year's share is then ranked from lowest to highest on a scale from 1 to 12. Rankings are aggregated for the two six-year periods, 1970-75 and 1976-81. A non-parametric test, the Wilcoxon-Mann-Whitney (W) test, is employed to detect whether a statistically significant change in the average of the market shares occurred between the two sample periods. This non-parametric test is employed largely because the sample size is small. (Appendix A provides a more detailed rationale for the test and an explanation of the procedures used.)

Against a null hypothesis (that no statistically significant change in market shares occurred), we test two alternative hypotheses: (1) market shares increased; and (2) market shares declined. The null hypothesis is rejected at the 5 percent significance level—that is, when there is a 95 percent probability that market shares either increased or declined. Special instances, where an alternative hypothesis could have been accepted at a slightly lower level of significance, are noted.

*Export and import data are derived from IMF sources. A complete set of tables for the market share analysis is included as Appendix C to the draft of this study submitted to the U.S. Department of State, Office of External Research. A copy can be obtained from the authors.

A common perception, confirmed by our review of aggregate data in Chapter 1, is that Japan has outperformed the United States in African export markets, while the United States has become a more important market for African exports. In the statistical tests of this study we shall test the hypotheses that after 1975 (1) the Japanese share in African imports increased while the U.S. share declined; and (2) the United States became a more important market for African exports. The first hypothesis would require a stronger performance on the part of Japan than might appear true at first sight. Most African countries are oil importers and were faced with a rapidly increasing oil import burden after 1973. Accordingly, one would expect the share of oil-exporting states in their market to rise, leaving little room for non-oil exporters to increase their market share. If Japan is found to have been successful in maintaining its market share, it would represent a major achievement. A confirmation of hypothesis (1) would testify to a particularly impressive export performance on the part of Japan.

Since Nigeria and South Africa are pivotal in determining the directions of African trade, we use country groupings in some of our statistical tests which exclude them. Likewise, by testing the economic relations of the United States and Japan with various regional groupings such as the Francophone and Anglophone states and with specific countries of particular economic importance, we can more carefully assess the comparative performance of the two countries. African countries were divided into the following groupings (the composition of the groupings is reported in Appendix B):

> Africa
> Africa excluding Nigeria
> Africa excluding South Africa
> Africa excluding Nigeria and South Africa
> Commonwealth Africa
> East Africa (Kenya, Tanzania, and Uganda)
> Francophone Africa
> Least Developed Africa
> Non-Oil Francophone Africa
> Oil Africa
> Ivory Coast
> Kenya

Nigeria
Senegal
South Africa
Zaire and Zambia
Zambia

RESULTS OF MARKET-SHARE ANALYSIS

U.S. and Japanese Shares in African Exports. Tables 2-7 and 2-8 present data on the U.S. and Japanese shares in African exports and (for purposes of comparison) in country groupings within Africa for 1970-75 and 1976-81. Table 2-7 shows that the United

Table 2-7

AVERAGE UNITED STATES SHARES IN AFRICAN EXPORTS,
1970-75 AND 1976-81
(Percent)

Country Grouping or Country	1970-75	1976-81	Significant Change
Africa	12.62%	21.22%	Upward
Africa excluding Nigeria	9.56	12.20	Upward
Africa excluding South Africa	14.30	26.76	Upward
Africa excluding Nigeria and South Africa	10.66	14.76	Upward
Commonwealth Africa	15.48	34.57	Upward
East Africa	9.73	10.18	None
Francophone Africa	8.67	11.99	Upward
Least Developed Africa	10.35	12.66	Upward
Non-Oil Francophone Africa	7.75	10.74	Upward
Oil Africa[a]	21.58	39.64	Upward
Ivory Coast	12.97	11.45	None
Kenya	4.58	4.54	None
Nigeria	21.76	42.16	Upward
Senegal	0.40	0.18	Downward
South Africa	7.27	8.98	Upward
Zaire and Zambia	2.43	11.50	Upward
Zambia	0.44	11.49	Upward

Source: Calculated from IMF, *Direction of Trade Statistics Yearbook*, 1975-80.

[a]Nigeria and Gabon.

Table 2-8

AVERAGE JAPANESE SHARES IN AFRICAN EXPORTS,
1970-75 AND 1976-81
(Percent)

Country Grouping or Country	1970-75	1976-81	Significant Change
Africa	6.88%	3.95%	Downward
Africa excluding Nigeria	7.85	5.45	Downward
Africa excluding South Africa	5.77	2.71	Downward
Africa excluding Nigeria and South Africa	6.70	4.43	Downward
Commonwealth Africa	7.05	2.22	Downward
East Africa	4.43	2.78	Downward
Francophone Africa	3.15	2.84	None
Least Developed Africa	6.57	4.68	Downward
Non-Oil Francophone Africa	3.37	3.32	None
Oil Africa[a]	3.81	0.70	Downward
Ivory Coast	1.67	2.08	None[b]
Kenya	2.11	1.12	Downward
Nigeria	3.03	0.49	Downward
Senegal	1.25	2.13	Upward
South Africa	10.68	6.79	Downward
Zaire and Zambia	13.08	8.58	Downward
Zambia	21.11	18.55	None[c]

Source: Same as Table 2-7.

[a]Nigeria and Gabon.
[b]Increase at the 6.6 percent significance level.
[c]Decrease at the 6.6 percent significance level.

States purchased a larger *share* of the exports of most African countries and groupings by the late 1970s than during the early 1970s. The increases are accounted for primarily by increases in the value of purchases of petroleum, minerals, and tropical products. The only exception to this pattern is Senegal, where the U.S. share of exports declined. The exports of East Africa and Ivory Coast to the United States displayed no statistically significant changes during the periods under study.

In contrast, the share of Japan in total African exports and in the exports of most African groupings declined. Senegal was the only exception. The explanation is that Japan increased its purchases of phosphates during a period when the European share of exports was affected by a decline in production of groundnuts, traditionally the most valuable Senegalese export to Europe. Japan's share in the exports of Francophone states and of Zambia showed no changes. Japan's apparent lack of interest in African exports stems in part from the fact that many of the goods which the Africans offer can be found closer to home and often with more stable sources of supply. This is certainly the case with petroleum and coal, as well as many tropical products such as cocoa and coffee, which Japan purchases in increasing quantities from Latin America. As we shall discuss in Chapter 3, although Japan has shown an increasing interest in African raw materials over the last decade, this has yet to be reflected in major investments and purchases (other than from South Africa).

U.S. and Japanese Shares in African Imports. Data on the shares of the United States and Japan in African imports are presented in Tables 2-9 and 2-10. The U.S. share declined or remained unchanged for all of the African groupings during the 1970s. For the continent as a whole, the U.S. share in the African market was unchanged at the 5 percent significance level but declined when the significance level is lowered to 6.6 percent. While there are several categories in which no change is observed, there is not a single African country or grouping where a statistically significant increase in the U.S. share of the market was recorded. In the largest Black African economy—Nigeria—the U.S. market share suffered a resounding decline. Reductions in U.S. shares of African imports were also recorded in Francophone Africa.

The Japanese performance compares favorably with that of the United States. Throughout the 1970s, higher petroleum prices necessitated that an increasing share of export earnings of most African countries be used to pay for oil imports. To record no changes in its share of African markets—as Japan did—indicates a relatively good performance, and almost certainly reflects substantially increased Japanese sales. Moreover, in Oil Africa, the Ivory Coast, and Senegal, the Japanese share of African imports increased in a statistically significant manner. Only in Zaire and Zambia (which account for the decreased share of imports in the Africa excluding Nigeria and South Africa grouping) did the Japanese market share decline. This comes as no surprise in view of the severe constraints on balance of payments

21

Table 2-9

AVERAGE U.S. SHARES IN AFRICAN IMPORTS, 1970-75 AND 1976-81
(Percent)

Country Grouping or Country	1970-75	1976-81	Significant Change
Africa	11.10%	10.03%	None[b]
Africa excluding Nigeria	11.00	10.21	Downward
Africa excluding South Africa	9.07	8.20	None[b]
Africa excluding Nigeria and South Africa	8.40	7.41	Downward
Commonwealth Africa	9.63	8.65	None
East Africa	6.33	5.42	None
Francophone Africa	7.61	6.40	Downward
Least Developed Africa	6.09	5.95	None
Non-Oil Francophone Africa	7.63	6.46	Downward
Oil Africa[a]	11.43	9.25	Downward
Ivory Coast	7.31	6.60	None
Kenya	7.10	6.45	None
Nigeria	12.06	9.39	Downward
Senegal	6.33	5.82	None
South Africa	15.17	15.84	None
Zaire and Zambia	9.55	9.57	None
Zambia	7.44	8.16	None

Source: Same as Table 2-7.

[a]Nigeria and Gabon.
[b]Decrease at the 6.6 percent significance level.

which Zaire and Zambia have faced in the past few years. Their ability to import has been severely curtailed by depressed world copper prices coupled with greatly increased petroleum import bills.

U.S. and Japanese Performance Compared to the EC. Because the EC is a major actor in African trade flows, representing nearly half of export and import purchases for most African countries, it is useful to compare the performance of the United States and Japan with that of the EC. Table 2-11 shows a summary of the statistically significant changes in the shares of the three trading partners in

Table 2-10

AVERAGE JAPANESE SHARES IN AFRICAN IMPORTS,
1970-75 AND 1976-81
(Percent)

Country Grouping or Country	1970-75	1976-81	Significant Change
Africa	7.73%	8.05%	None
Africa excluding Nigeria	7.53	9.14	None
Africa excluding South Africa	6.79	7.35	None
Africa excluding Nigeria and South Africa	6.24	5.49	Downward
Commonwealth Africa	8.29	9.30	None[b]
East Africa	8.46	9.08	None
Francophone Africa	3.90	4.07	None
Least Developed Africa	5.97	6.01	None
Non-Oil Francophone Africa	4.10	4.12	None
Oil Africa[a]	7.53	9.56	Upward
Ivory Coast	3.25	5.31	Upward
Kenya	10.05	10.06	None
Nigeria	8.81	10.37	None[b]
Senegal	0.41	0.98	Upward
South Africa	9.61	10.39	None
Zaire and Zambia	7.64	3.98	Downward
Zambia	7.71	4.30	Downward

Source: Same as Table 2-7.

[a]Nigeria and Gabon.
[b]Increase at the 6.6 percent significance level.

the exports and imports of the principal African groupings. The table highlights the relatively poor performance of the United States in the African market. At the 6.6 percent significance level the U.S. share of African imports declined significantly in all of the groupings. By recording no change in most markets, Japan and the EC have out-performed the United States. Only in the less important African markets—Africa excluding Nigeria and South Africa—did the EC record a better performance than Japan. Moreover, the United States absorbed an increasing share of the exports of all African groupings while the shares of Japan and the EC for the most part declined.

Table 2-11

COMPARISON OF STATISTICALLY SIGNIFICANT CHANGES IN U.S., JAPANESE, AND EC SHARES IN AFRICAN EXPORTS AND IMPORTS BETWEEN 1970-75 AND 1976-81

	Shares held by		
Grouping	United States	Japan	EC
African Exports			
Africa	Upward	Downward	Downward
Africa excluding Nigeria	Upward	Downward	Downward
Africa excluding South Africa	Upward	Downward	Downward
Africa excluding Nigeria and South Africa	Upward	Downward	None
African Imports			
Africa	None[a]	None	None
Africa excluding Nigeria	Downward	None	None
Africa excluding South Africa	None[a]	None	None
Africa excluding Nigeria and South Africa	Downward	Downward	None

Source: Same as Table 2-7.

[a] Decrease at the 6.6 percent significance level.

CHANGES IN THE BALANCE OF TRADE

Changes in the market shares of the United States and Japan are reflected in divergent developments in their balance of trade with Africa. Japan's success in selling to the African market while decreasing its share of exports from the continent has enabled it to run a sizable trade surplus in recent years. The United States, by contrast, has run a consistent deficit.

The balance of trade can be viewed from two perspectives—the export and import position of either of two trading partners. Traditionally in an analysis of the balance of trade, exports are counted f.o.b. and imports are counted c.i.f.; we shall follow this method. In cases where trade imbalances are very small, the inclusion or exclusion of c.i.f. charges can make a difference in the final trade account position: it is possible to have the somewhat anomalous situation in which both sides are running a deficit simultaneously. In this section we shall look at the U.S. and Japanese trade account with Africa from the perspectives of both the United States and Japan, on the one hand, and of Africa on the other.

BALANCE OF TRADE FROM THE U.S. AND JAPANESE PERSPECTIVE

The United States has run sizable and steady deficits with Africa since 1972 (see Figures 2-1 and 2-2). Imports from Nigeria account for a large part of the deficits; when Nigeria is excluded, the trade imbalance is less pronounced. Nevertheless, the magnitude of the numbers is revealing. The U.S. deficit with Non-Oil Africa was in the billions of dollars in the late 1970s. Trade deficits of such magnitudes cannot but be of concern to U.S. policymakers—particularly when the United States appears to have been less successful than Japan in penetrating the market of Nigeria, which is its major source of African imports.

In contrast, the Japanese trade balance with Africa has showed considerable improvement in the past few years. A marked movement from deficits in the first half of the 1970s to surpluses in the latter half of the decade is clear from Figure 2-1. The only exception to this pattern is a small deficit in 1979, due largely to an increase in the prices of African primary products (and thus in the value of Japanese imports) at a time when many African countries were cutting their imports of manufactured goods because of an increase in their oil bills. However, the Japanese move into the red was quickly reversed in 1980 and 1981.

Sales to Nigeria play a very important role in keeping the Japanese trade position with Africa as strong as it is. When Nigeria is excluded (as in Figure 2-2), the Japanese balance of trade with the rest of the continent falls slightly into deficit. However, the deficits are very small. In fact, they are so minor that if freight and insurance charges were excluded, Japan would be perceived as running a surplus.

25

Figure 2-1

Figure 2-1

U.S. AND JAPANESE BALANCE OF TRADE WITH AFRICA, 1970-81

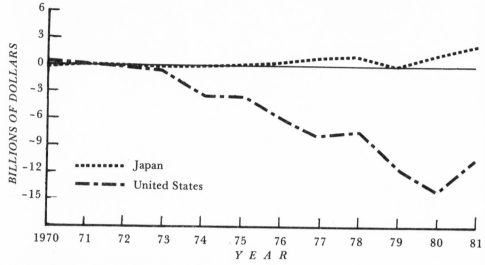

Source: Appendix C, Table C-3.

Figure 2-2

U.S. AND JAPANESE BALANCE OF TRADE WITH AFRICA
EXCLUDING NIGERIA, 1970-81

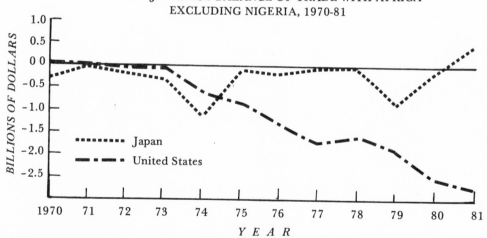

Source: Appendix C, Table C-2.

BALANCE OF TRADE FROM THE AFRICAN PERSPECTIVE

African countries in recent years have run a large trade surplus with the United States and a trade deficit with Japan, the Organization of Petroleum Exporting Countries—OPEC (except Nigeria), and the EC (see Figure 2-3). The Africans appear to be earning foreign exchange in the U.S. market and using it to purchase manufactured goods and oil imports from other countries, primarily the EC, Japan, and the OPEC countries. When Nigeria is excluded (as in Figure 2-4), the magnitude of the imbalance is reduced, but Africa still runs a balance-of-trade surplus with the United States and deficits with its other major trading partners.

CHANGES IN COMPOSITION OF TRADE

Our analysis of aggregate trade flows has pointed to a number of significant differences in the development of trade relations between the United States and Africa and Japan and Africa over the 1970s. A more detailed investigation of the composition of trade between the parties is necessary in order to attempt to account for these differences.

IMPORT COMPOSITION

U.S. imports from Africa are dominated by fuel (Table 2-12). Surprisingly, the next most important category is manufactured goods, which are derived for the most part from South Africa.

Japan's imports from Africa largely follow a predictable pattern. As Table 2-13 shows, most Japanese imports are raw materials and foodstuffs. Particularly important are such minerals as copper, cobalt, manganese, uranium, and mineral fuels such as petroleum and coal. Coffee, cocoa, and feedgrains are the most important foodstuffs. Somewhat surprising is the large share of manufactured goods in Japanese imports from the continent, but a major part of this figure is accounted for by the re-export of ships from Liberia. Table 2-14 provides a more detailed breakdown of Japanese import composition by principal trading partner. Although South Africa remains the principal source of Japanese imports from the continent, Japan's purchases from South Africa are predominantly raw materials and foodstuffs.

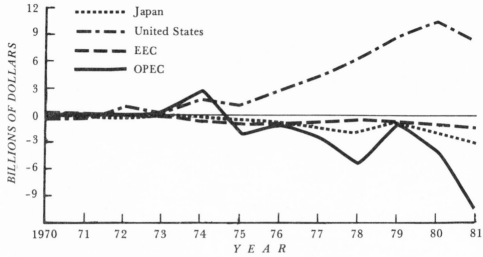

Figure 2-3

AFRICA'S BALANCE OF TRADE WITH MAJOR TRADING
PARTNERS, 1970-81

Source: Appendix C, Table C-3.

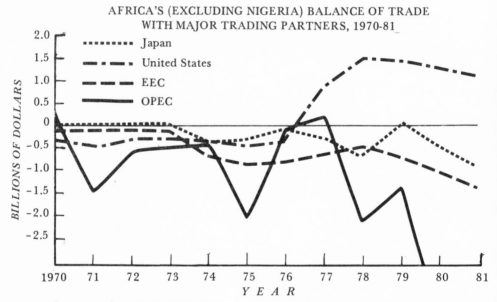

Figure 2-4

AFRICA'S (EXCLUDING NIGERIA) BALANCE OF TRADE
WITH MAJOR TRADING PARTNERS, 1970-81

Source: Appendix C, Table C-4.

Table 2-12

COMPOSITION OF U.S. IMPORTS FROM AFRICA BY SITC CATEGORY,[a] 1980

SITC Category	Africa Volume (Millions of dollars)	Africa Share[b] (Percent)	Nigeria Volume (Millions of dollars)	Nigeria Share (Percent)	South Africa Volume (Millions of dollars)	South Africa Share (Percent)	Africa excluding Nigeria and South Africa Volume (Millions of dollars)	Africa excluding Nigeria and South Africa Share (Percent)
Food, beverages, and tobacco	$ 1,388.2	7.7%	$ 71.1	0.7%	$ 141.0	4.2%	$ 1,176.1	31.2%
Fuels	12,427.3	69.1	10,802.8	99.1	25.6	0.8	1,598.9	42.5
Raw Materials	597.2	3.3	11.8	0.1	236.3	7.1	349.1	9.3
Chemicals	56.0	0.3	0.1	—	46.2	1.4	9.7	0.3
Manufactured goods	2,435.5	13.5	13.3	0.1	1,836.8	55.3	585.4	15.6
Machinery and transport equipment	40.7	0.2	0.1	—	33.7	1.0	6.9	0.2
Miscellaneous manufactures and unclassified	1,044.4	5.8	6.0	—	1,001.2	30.2	37.2	1.0
TOTAL	17,989.2	100.0	10,905.1	100.0	3,320.5	100.0	3,763.6	100.0

Source: U.S. Department of Commerce, Bureau of Census, U.S. Imports: World Trade by Commodity Groupings, 1980.

[a] Standard International Trade Classification.
[b] Percentage shares refer to columns, not rows. They may not add up to 100 owing to rounding errors.

Table 2-13

COMPOSITION OF JAPANESE IMPORTS FROM AFRICA BY SITC CATEGORY, 1981

SITC Category	Africa		Nigeria		South Africa		Africa excluding Nigeria and South Africa	
	Volume (Millions of dollars)	Share[a] (Percent)	Volume (Millions of dollars)	Share (Percent)	Volume (Millions of dollars)	Share (Percent)	Volume (Millions of dollars)	Share (Percent)
Food, beverages, and tobacco	$ 732.8	21.5%	$ 6.6	1.9%	$ 432.2	25.0%	$ 294.0	21.8%
Fuels	621.4	18.2	331.2	97.3	263.5	15.2	26.7	2.0
Raw materials	766.2	22.4	2.1	0.6	459.9	26.6	304.2	22.6
Chemicals	64.0	1.9	0	0	61.5	3.6	2.5	0.2
Manufactured goods	881.5	25.8	0	0	473.3	27.4	408.2	30.3
Machinery and transport equipment	73.4	2.1	0	0	1.3	0.1	72.1	5.4
Miscellaneous manufactures and unclassified	276.8	8.1	0.4	0.1	36.7	2.1	239.7	17.8
TOTAL	3,416.1	100.0	340.4	100.0	1,728.3	100.0	1,347.4	100.0

Source: JETRO, White Paper on International Trade, 1982.
[a]Percentage shares refer to columns, not rows. They may not add up to 100.0 owing to rounding errors.

Table 2-14

COMPOSITION OF JAPANESE IMPORTS FROM
LARGEST TRADING PARTNERS IN AFRICA, 1981

Trading Partner	Raw Materials[a]		Primary Foodstuffs[b]		Manufactures	Other
	Percent	Major Components	Percent	Major Components		
South Africa	73%	Iron, manganese, chromium, coal, platinum[c]	25%	Corn, sugar, fruits and vegetables	—	2%
Nigeria	98	Petroleum	2	Seafood	—	—
Kenya	67	Sisal, fluorspar	21	Corn, nuts	—	—
Sudan	100	Cotton	—		—	—
Tanzania	16	Sisal	70	Coffee	—	14
Ivory Coast	21	Cotton, wood	78	Cocoa, coffee	—	1
Zaire	98	Copper, Copper alloys	—		—	2
Ethiopia	19	Animal skins	80	Coffee	—	1
Zambia	99	Copper	1		—	—
Liberia	—		3		23%	74[d]
Ghana	55	Aluminum ingots	42	Cocoa	—	—

Source: Same as Table 2-13.

[a]Includes minerals and mineral fuels.
[b]As listed in JETRO data.
[c]Includes raw materials that have undergone processing.
[d]Transactions not classified.

EXPORT COMPOSITION

Of particular interest to policymakers is the evolution of the composition of exports from the United States and Japan to Africa over the last decade. If, as our analysis above suggests, Japan has been more successful in penetrating African markets in the 1970s, it is vital to ascertain the products involved and the extent to which these compete with U.S. exports.

Table 2-15 compares changes in the composition of U.S. and Japanese exports to Africa over the last decade. For the United States the most significant change has been an increase in its export share of food, beverages, and tobacco. This has been accompanied by a decline in the share of manufactured goods and machinery and transport equipment. For Japan, on the other hand, the most signif-

Table 2-15

COMPARISON OF U.S. AND JAPANESE EXPORTS TO AFRICA
BY SITC CATEGORY, 1970, 1975, 1980
(Percent)

SITC Category	U.S. Share			Japanese Share		
	1970	1975	1980	1970	1975	1980
Food, beverages, and tobacco	10.4%	11.7%	17.9%	2.6%	2.5%	3.5%
Fuels	1.8	1.4	1.7	0.0	0.0	0.0
Raw materials	3.9	4.4	6.2	0.4	0.5	0.6
Chemicals	9.2	7.4	10.2	3.7	3.2	2.6
Manufactured goods	14.8	14.5	11.8	50.2	39.6	28.6
Machinery and transport equipment	52.0	53.4	44.1	40.3	51.9	61.6
Miscellaneous manufactures and unclassified	8.0	7.1	8.0	2.8	2.3	3.1

Sources: U.S. Department of Commerce, Bureau of Census, *U.S. Exports: World Trade by Commodity Groupings*, 1971, 1976, 1981; JETRO, *White Paper on International Trade*, 1971, 1976, 1982.

icant change has been a rapid growth in the share of machinery and transport equipment, accompanied by a decline in the share of manufactured goods. It must be remembered that these figures represent changes in the *share* of exports; a decline in share does not imply a decline in the real value of exports. As Table 2-16 shows, the real value of Japanese exports of manufactured goods continued to rise over the decade. Table 2-16 must be interpreted with caution, however, since it focuses on rates of growth: a small absolute increase

Table 2-16

AVERAGE ANNUAL REAL RATES OF GROWTH OF U.S. AND JAPANESE EXPORTS TO AFRICA BY SITC CATEGORY, 1970-80[a]
(Percent)

SITC Category	U.S. Rate		Japanese Rate	
Food, beverages, and tobacco	22.4%	($990.1)[b]	21.6%	($174.0)
Fuels	7.8	(93.0)	0.0	(0)
Raw materials	19.9	(244.2)	25.1	(29.8)
Chemicals	10.9	(563.8)	6.5	(129.5)
Manufactured goods	5.0	(654.9)	3.4	(1422.1)
Machinery and transport equipment	6.0	(2440.5)	25.9	(3063.1)
Capital equipment	5.6		17.4	
Road equipment	2.3		26.5	
Miscellaneous manu- factures and unclassified	8.8	(433.3)	16.0	(154.1)
Total exports	8.8	(5529.5)	13.5	(4972.5)

Sources: U.S. Dept. of Commerce, Bureau of Census, *U.S. Exports: World Trade by Commodity Groupings*, 1970 and 1980; OECD, *Development Cooperation: 1982 Review* (Paris, 1982); JETRO, *White Paper on International Trade*, 1972 and 1982.

[a]Average annual rates of growth have been constructed in accordance with Organization for Economic Cooperation and Development (OECD) practice by use of a U.S. dollar index with base 1980=100.

[b]Figures in parentheses are export values (in millions of dollars) for the categories in 1980.

may be reflected in a large percentage change if the base figure was small. This explains the large percentage increase in Japan's exports of food, beverages, and tobacco, which are accounted for almost entirely by the sale of fish.

These caveats notwithstanding, Tables 2-15 and 2-16 provide some interesting comparisons between the U.S. and Japanese performance in African markets. By 1980 Japan was outselling the United States in African markets both for manufactured goods and for machinery and transport equipment. It is in the latter category that Japan's performance has been most impressive. In 1975 the United States was exporting machinery and transport equipment to a value of close to 50 percent more than the Japanese total ($1620 million in contrast to $1163 million). By 1980 the picture had reversed, with Japan exporting goods in this category to a value in excess of 50 percent of the U.S. equivalent.

Japan's phenomenal success in exporting machinery and transport equipment to Africa is the result of a sustained drive to upgrade and diversify its exports—especially toward products with a higher value-added domestically. Whereas in the first half of the 1970s these consisted in large part of manufactured goods (SITC category 6)—especially steel and textiles—the exports in 1980 were more sophisticated products of machinery and transport equipment (SITC category 7)—particularly heavy equipment, industrial plant, and telecommunications machinery. Also important in this category are Japan's exports of transportation equipment.

This dramatic transformation of the U.S. and Japanese shares of the African market for machinery and transport equipment warrants further examination. Table 2-17 provides a detailed comparison of the exports of the two countries for this category in 1980. Given the success of Japan in penetrating the domestic U.S. market for radios, TVs, and (more recently) automobiles, it is scarcely surprising that Japanese exports of these goods to Africa considerably exceed those from the United States. There must be some concern, however, for U.S. automakers regarding the extent to which their Japanese competitors have come to dominate the African market, and, in more recent years, the Japanese move to establish assembly plants in Africa (reflected in the sales of chassis and motor vehicle parts).

Although the United States continues to outsell Japan in providing "capital" equipment to the African market, Japan is rapidly

Table 2-17

COMPARISON OF U.S. AND JAPANESE EXPORTS
OF MACHINERY AND TRANSPORT EQUIPMENT (SITC CATEGORY 7)
TO AFRICA BY SITC SUBCATEGORY, 1980
(Millions of dollars)

SITC Subcategory	United States		Japan	
"Capital" Equipment	$1654.6	(67.8%)	$ 777.3	(25.4%)
Internal combustion	148.1		105.9	
Agricultural, textile, mining,				
construction	694.1		163.5	
Metal-working	49.5		66.3	
Heating/cooling/cargo handling	418.3		154.7	
Office machines	134.8		44.0	
Telecommunications	72.7		131.9	
Heavy electrical	137.1		111.0	
Road Transport	288.4	(11.8%)	1465.2	(47.8%)
Passenger cars	12.4		328.2	
Trucks/special vehicles	109.8		165.5	
Buses	12.0		213.8	
Chassis/motor vehicle parts	141.4		410.5	
Motorcycles	12.8		347.2	
TV/Radios//Tape Recorders	8.5	(0.3%)	339.3	(11.1%)
TV	N.A.		49.0	
Radios	N.A.		189.2	
Tape recorders	N.A.		101.1	
Other[a]	489.0	(20.0%)	483.7	(15.8%)
TOTAL	2440.5		3065.5	

Sources: U.S. Department of Commerce, Bureau of Census, *U.S. Exports:
World Trade by Commodity Groupings,* 1980; JETRO, *White Paper
on International Trade,* 1982.

[a]For the United States this subcategory included mainly household machinery, other electrical equipment, ships,and airplanes; for Japan it included mainly
household machinery, rail equipment, and ships (excluding sales to Liberia).

catching up. Whereas U.S. sales in this category rose from $1135 million in 1975 to $1654.6 million in 1980, those of Japan increased from $220.1 million to $777.3 million—a larger absolute as well as a larger percentage increase. By 1980 Japanese sales of metal-working machinery and telecommunications equipment exceeded those of the United States, and they were rapidly approaching the figure for U.S. heavy electrical machinery exports.

Also of concern is Japan's relative success in penetrating the Black African market (see Tables 2-18 and 2-19). Over 70 percent of Japan's exports to the Nigerian market in 1981 were composed of goods in the category of machinery and transport equipment, which also accounted for over 50 percent of sales to Africa excluding Nigeria and South Africa. In total, Black Africa accounted for 62 percent of Japanese sales of "capital" equipment to sub-Saharan Africa in that year. In contrast, sales of machinery and transport equipment comprised only 37 percent of U.S. sales to Nigeria in 1980. South Africa accounted for 54 percent of U.S. sales of "capital" equipment to sub-Saharan Africa in that year. A similar pattern is evident for other items in the category of machinery and transport equipment: for Japan, Black Africa provided more than half of the market; for the United States, South Africa accounted for more than half of its exports in this category. For manufactured goods the situation is even more exaggerated: South Africa accounted for over two thirds of U.S. exports but less than one third of Japan's. Clearly the United States is losing out to its Japanese competitors in the growing markets of Black Africa. It is quite staggering that barely more than 2 percent of U.S. exports to Africa excluding Nigeria and South Africa were manufactured goods.

There are only two categories of goods in which U.S. exports to Africa over the last decade have grown more rapidly than those of Japan. The first is chemicals, over two thirds of which in 1980 were purchased in South Africa. The second is food, beverages, and tobacco, which in 1980 accounted for approximately one third of all U.S. exports to Black Africa. At first sight, the figure for the latter category might appear to be testimony to the efficiency of U.S. agriculture and the success of its export drive. However, fully 30 percent of U.S. exports in this category in 1980 were paid for by Public Law (PL) 480 transactions, over one half of which consisted of grants to recipient African states.

Table 2-18

COMPOSITION OF U.S. EXPORTS TO AFRICA BY SITC CATEGORY, 1980

SITC Category	Africa		Nigeria		South Africa		Africa excluding Nigeria and South Africa	
	Volume (Millions of dollars)	Share[a] (Percent)	Volume (Millions of dollars)	Share (Percent)	Volume (Millions of dollars)	Share (Percent)	Volume (Millions of dollars)	Share (Percent)
Food, beverages and tobacco[b]	$ 990.1	17.9%	$ 327.6	29.0%	$ 79.9	2.9%	$ 582.6	34.6%
Fuels	93.0	1.7	15.7	1.4	43.2	15.9	34.1	2.0
Raw materials[c]	344.1	6.2	30.4	2.7	155.7	5.7	158.0	9.4
Chemicals[d]	563.8	10.2	88.4	7.8	382.9	14.1	92.5	5.5
Manufactured goods[e]	654.9	11.8	176.0	15.6	444.4	16.4	34.5	2.1
Machinery and transport equipment	2,440.5	44.1	416.8	36.9	1,324.1	48.7	699.6	41.5
Miscellaneous manufactures and unclassified[f]	443.3	8.0	73.6	6.5	286.7	10.6	83.0	4.9
TOTAL	5,529.6	100.0	1,128.5	100.0	2,716.9	100.0	1,684.2	100.0

Source: U.S. Department of Commerce, Bureau of Census, U.S. Exports: World Trade by Commodity Groupings, 1980.

[a]Percentage shares refer to columns, not rows. They may not add up to 100.0 owing to rounding errors.
[b]Includes food aid under PL 480.
[c]Mainly wood pulp, lumber, synthetic rubber, and bauxite.
[d]Mainly organic chemicals, pesticides, metallic compounds, synthetic resins, and fuel additives.
[e]Mainly paper products, yarn, and woven fabrics.
[f]Mainly measuring instruments, film, and books.

Table 2-19

COMPOSITION OF JAPANESE EXPORTS TO AFRICA BY SITC CATEGORY, 1981

SITC Category	Africa		Nigeria		South Africa		Africa excluding Nigeria and South Africa	
	Volume (Millions of dollars)	Share[a] (Percent)	Volume (Millions of dollars)	Share (Percent)	Volume (Millions of dollars)	Share (Percent)	Volume (Millions of dollars)	Share (Percent)
Food, beverages, and tobacco[b]	$ 187.6	3.3%	$ 95.9	4.5%	$ 31.8	1.4%	$ 59.9	4.5%
Fuels	0	0	0	0	0	0	0	0
Raw materials	22.7	0.4	1.5	0.1	21.8	1.0	0	0
Chemicals[c]	130.8	2.3	28.5	1.3	71.9	3.2	30.4	2.3
Manufactured goods[d]	1,381.5	24.3	499.9	23.5	446.4	20.1	435.2	32.5
Machinery and transport equipment	3,814.8[f]	67.1	1,512.0	71.2	1,574.0	70.8	728.8[f]	54.4
Miscellaneous manufactures and unclassified[e]	136.4	2.4	13.0	0.6	74.1	3.3	49.3	3.7
TOTAL	5,685.3	100.0	2,122.8	100.0	2,222.0	100.0	1,340.5	100.0

Source: JETRO, White Paper on International Trade, 1982.

[a]Percentage shares refer to columns, not rows. They may not add up to 100.0 owing to rounding errors.
[b]Primarily fish.
[c]Primarily plastics and artificial resins.
[d]Primarily iron and steel, metal products, and textiles.
[e]Primarily scientific and optical instruments.
[f]Excludes exports of ships to Liberia.

CONCLUSIONS

In this chapter we have pointed to a number of alarming trends in the development of U.S. and Japanese commerce with Africa over the last decade. Whereas Japan has generally been successful in maintaining its shares of African markets, the U.S. share in most cases has declined in a statistically significant manner. This decline has been a major cause of the burgeoning U.S. trade deficit with the continent; the deficit is not merely the result of increased imports, but also stems from the failure of the United States to maintain its share of markets in sub-Saharan Africa other than South Africa.

What must be of particular concern to U.S. policymakers is the failure of the United States to keep pace with Japanese sales of machinery and transport equipment to Black Africa. The failure is particularly evident in the Nigerian market, where Japan has enjoyed considerable success, largely financed by Nigerian petroleum sales to the United States. Our analysis of course cannot tell us what factors account for the relative success of Japanese exporters—whether it is simply a matter of superior products, more competitive pricing, or more aggressive sales techniques, or whether Japanese exporters benefit from government support in the African market which is not available to their U.S. competitors. In the following chapters we shall examine various aspects of Japan's marketing strategy—its investment and aid relations with Africa (Chapters 3 and 4) and government assistance to exporters (Chapter 5).

Chapter 3

JAPANESE OVERSEAS INVESTMENTS

Changes in the pattern of Japan's foreign direct investment (FDI) have flowed directly from the structural transformation of its domestic economy. Until the mid-1960s Japan was only a minor international investor with modest sums invested in the establishment of sales offices overseas and in import-substitution industries (primarily in Latin America). Even in Asia Japan's ventures were on a small scale since most were designed to cater to what were then quite limited domestic markets. During this period most investment was directed toward the transformation of the domestic economy from one based on labor-intensive production of light manufactures (notably textiles) to capital-intensive heavy and chemical industries and to research-intensive light manufacturing such as electronics. By the mid-1960s heavy industrialization was completed, thereby transforming Japan's factor endowments. Successful industrialization created labor shortages and rapidly pushed up real wages; in the process Japan's competitiveness in the export of labor-intensive products was undermined.

Declining shares of the world market in light manufactured products as a result of loss of competitiveness was one factor which encouraged investment overseas—to take advantage of the abundant labor supply positions of many of Japan's neighbors. Several other factors served to "push" investment overseas, including increasing concern over the environmental costs of heavy industry and the rapid increase in domestic land values. A number of factors specific to potential hosts simultaneously combined to attract Japanese investment—most notably the availability of raw materials, on which Japan was becoming increasingly dependent, and overseas government policies which offered incentives to foreign investors. The latter were of both positive and negative forms—positive in the provision of such advantages as tax holidays and generous depreciation allowances,

40

negative by way of protectionist legislation designed to promote local manufacturing through import substitution.

Increased overseas investment was facilitated by the emergence of an export surplus in 1965. This enabled the government to relax controls on capital outflow. In 1969 the system of screening investment proposals on a case-by-case basis was supplemented by automatic approval for investments of less than $200,000; in 1970 this limit was raised to $1 million; it was eliminated entirely in the following year. Indeed 1971 proved to be a watershed in the history of Japan's FDI, in large part because it represented the end of the Bretton Woods monetary system and the subsequent devaluation of the dollar, causing a rapid appreciation of the yen—and thereby an increase in the volume of overseas assets that could be obtained with any given yen investment. Below we shall discuss Japan's record in FDI, consider the role of its trading companies, and assess Japanese perceptions of the African investment environment.

FOREIGN DIRECT INVESTMENT RECORD

As Table 3-1 shows, Japanese cumulative FDI doubled in value from 1968 to 1971 and then doubled again by 1973. One of the most striking features is the ability that Japanese industry has displayed to maintain rates of growth of FDI averaging over 20 percent per annum despite an ever-increasing numerical base. But this high rate of growth notwithstanding, total Japanese investment lags far behind that of the United States. Although growing at a slower rate each year, total U.S. investment still increases by a substantially larger absolute figure than that of Japan (see Table E-1 in Appendix E).*

*In a comparison of Japanese and U.S. FDI, a variety of problems are encountered arising from the different definitions of FDI employed by the two governments. The official statistics of Japanese overseas investments are broken down into five categories: securities investments, direct overseas loans, acquisition of real estate, establishment of branch offices, and direct overseas investment (by firms as Japanese corporate bodies without their being incorporated locally). The inclusion of direct overseas loans is not the normal practice in measuring FDI since such loans do not provide ownership or managerial control. The U.S. Department of Commerce defines U.S. private foreign investment as the net book value of equity and loans to foreign affiliates which control at least 10 percent of voting securities.

Table 3-1

VALUE OF JAPAN'S TOTAL FOREIGN DIRECT INVESTMENT (FDI),
1951-81

Fiscal Year	FDI (Millions of dollars)	Cumulative Value (Millions of dollars)	Growth Rate (Percent)
1951-61	$ 447	$ 447	
1962	98	545	21.8%
1963	126	671	23.1
1964	119	790	17.7
1965	159	949	20.1
1966	227	1176	23.9
1967	275	1451	23.4
1968	557	2008	38.4
1969	665	2673	33.1
1970	904	3577	33.8
1971	858	4435	24.0
1972	2338	6773	52.7
1973	3494	10267	51.6
1974	2396	12663	23.3
1975	3280	15943	25.9
1976	3462	19405	21.7
1977	2806	22211	14.5
1978	4598	26809	20.7
1979	4995	31804	18.6
1980	4693	36497	14.8
1981	8906	45403	24.4

Source: 1951-77: Terutomo Ozawa, *Multinationalism, Japanese Style* (Princeton: Princeton University Press, 1979), p. 12; 1978-81: Japan, Ministry of International Trade and Industry (MITI), *Direct Overseas Investments from Japanese Companies* (annual).

Africa is the least favored of the regions in the geographical distribution of Japan's FDI (see Table 3-2). Its share of Japan's total overseas investment rose from 2.1 percent in 1971 to 4.4 percent in 1981, but the more recent figure includes investments in North Africa, particularly Libya. Sub-Saharan Africa accounts for less than 1.7 percent of the cumulative total of Japan's postwar overseas investment. This translates to only $1,417.6 million.[1] Africa merited only one paragraph in a recent comprehensive survey of Japanese multi-nationalism—a book of 289 pages![2] It is worth noting in passing, however, that whereas Africa's share in total Japanese investments has been rising, its share in total U.S. FDI (and in U.S. FDI in developing countries) has been falling since the early 1970s (see Tables E-2—E-5 in Appendix E).

Detailed figures on the overseas activities of Japanese corporations are available from both government and private sources (in marked contrast to the United States). Table 3-3 provides a country-by-country breakdown of the major Japanese investments in sub-Saharan Africa. A cursory glance reveals Japan's heavy concentration in a limited number of countries. Over one half of the sub-Saharan African total is invested in Liberia, mainly in shipping companies (many of which remain 100 percent Japanese-owned). The other principal hosts are Niger, Zambia, and Zaire—in which Japan has interests in mining—and Nigeria, where Japanese investors have promoted

Table 3-2

GEOGRAPHICAL DISTRIBUTION OF JAPANESE FOREIGN
DIRECT INVESTMENT, 1981
(*Percent of total value*)

North America	Latin America	Asia	Middle and Near East	Europe	Africa[a]	Oceania
27.1%	16.2%	29.0%	5.2%	11.6%	4.4%	6.5%

Source: Calculated from MITI, "Direct Overseas Investment from Japanese Companies in Fiscal 1981," *News from MITI*, 23 June 1982, Table 4.

[a]Includes North Africa.

Table 3-3

JAPANESE INVESTMENT IN BLACK AFRICA: BREAKDOWN BY SELECTED COUNTRIES, 1951-69–1981

(Thousands of dollars)

Country	1951-69[a]	1970	1971	1972	1973	1974	1975	1976	1977	1978	1979	1980	1981	Total
Cameroon	$1,308 (2)[b]												$ 39 (2)	$ 1,573 (4)
Ethiopia	3,732 (7)	330 (2)		$ 243 (2)	$2,525 (2)									6,831 (13)
Gabon	430 (2)	18 (1)	$111			$ 250 (1)	$ 441 (1)	$ 7,520 (2)	$10,248 (3)		$ 6,204 (1)	$ 6,594 (4)	29,697 (15)	61,518 (30)
Gambia		192 (1)	200 (1)		1,410 (2)									1,802 (4)
Ghana	50 (1)			288 (2)	21 (1)			720						1,080 (4)
Guinea				1,020 (1)	370 (3)	2,715 (4)	848 (3)	2,378 (1)						7,332 (12)
Ivory Coast	585 (2)	234 (1)	41 (1)		3,218 (2)	757 (2)	452 (1)	417 (2)			44			5,750 (11)
Kenya	2,408 (11)	1,052 (4)	130 (1)	258 (4)	1,832 (4)	1,099 (5)	527 (1)		290 (3)		722 (4)			8,322 (37)
Liberia	90 (2)	6,041 (4)	233 (5)	10,344 (14)	3,347 (23)	22,291 (40)	86,291 (48)	145,254 (64)	95,184 (35)	$181,604 (34)	130,330 (37)	110,115 (40)	486,073 (68)	1,267,402 (414)
Madagascar	261 (3)	70	2,177 (4)	1 (1)	2,026 (5)	1,541 (4)	256 (2)		170 (1)	1,724 (1)	2,691 (3)	141 (1)		11,066 (25)
Mauritania			3,938 (2)		323 (1)									4,262 (3)
Mauritius	17 (1)	89 (1)		19		720 (1)				3,983 (1)	99	130 (1)		5,050 (5)
Mozambique										76 (1)	2,372 (1)	3,756 (1)	1,931 (1)	8,136 (4)
Namibia	364 (1)													364 (1)
Niger					1,265 (1)	1,181 (1)	6,023 (1)	31,333 (2)	3,571 (1)	17,778 (3)	11,760 (1)		4,430 (2)	77,344 (12)

Table 3-3 (cont.)

Country	1951-69[a]	1970	1971	1972	1973	1974	1975	1976	1977	1978	1979	1980	1981	Total
Nigeria	$9,419 (12)	$2,351 (3)	$8,085 (2)	$17,128 (6)	$20,882 (4)	$20,022 (5)	$34,042 (8)	$12,634 (3)	$4,802 (5)	$3,337 (8)	$8,751 (11)	$11,554 (7)	$1,009 (4)	$154,022 (78)
Rwanda	50 (1)					17					100 (1)			167 (2)
Senegal				1,276 (2)	359 (3)	2,026 (6)	2,230 (2)		588 (2)	1,241 (3)	63	69 (1)	57	7,914 (19)
Sierra Leone	50 (1)	100 (1)												150 (2)
Sudan	602 (2)				266	312 (1)	1,012	1,562						3,756 (3)
Swaziland				8 (1)			230 (1)		1,725 (1)	290 (1)	1,266			3,519 (4)
Tanzania	1,394 (8)	69	474 (1)	280	400 (1)	1,299 (1)		813 (1)	47 (1)	227 (1)	151 (2)	332 (2)		5,491 (18)
Uganda	234 (4)		36					240 (1)	34					547 (5)
Upper Volta							1,031 (2)	86 (1)				26 (1)		1,146 (4)
Zaire	13,603 (5)	3,096 (4)	6,685 (3)	2,536 (4)	67,338 (7)		57,693 (8)	68,781 (7)	14,000 (3)	7,430 (3)		3,700 (1)	11,500 (6)	256,344 (51)
Zambia	43,410 (3)	8 (1)			166 (2)	283 (2)	564 (4)					443	55,000 (2)	90,870 (14)
Zimbabwe	70 (1)												720 (1)	790 (2)

Source: MITI, internal document (mimeo).

[a]1951-69 cumulative total.

[b]Figures in parentheses are number of cases.

[c]A figure listed without a corresponding number of cases in parentheses represents additional investment by an existing firm.

import-substituting manufacturing industries. Together these five countries account for over 90 percent of Japan's sub-Saharan investment. A total of only $100 million has been invested in all other Black African countries. A number of surprising features stand out in the table—e.g., Japan has invested nearly as much in Mozambique as in Kenya, while language barriers have not prevented considerable activity in Francophone Africa.

Table 3-4 provides a breakdown of Japanese investments in Africa (including North Africa) by sector. The manufacturing sector, as would be expected, accounts for only a small percentage of total investments. However, the share of metals manufacturing has increased, replacing textiles as the most important subsector in Japanese manufacturing investments. In the non-manufacturing sector, the largest single category is "other"—presumably largely accounted for by Japanese shipping firms in Liberia. Next in importance is mining, which accounts for over 25 percent of total Japanese investment in Africa. In recent years the major growth areas have been metals manufacturing, with three new investments from 1979 to 1981 amounting to $58 million, and mining, with twenty-nine new investments in the same period with a value of $56 million. (Owing to a lack of data, it is difficult to provide a comparable analysis for the United States. Table E-6 provides a rudimentary breakdown of U.S. investment by sector in Africa in 1978; its most notable feature is the preponderant role of investments in petroleum.)

JAPANESE INVESTMENTS IN AFRICAN MINERALS

There are presently eleven major minerals ventures in Africa which involve substantial Japanese participation. These are listed in Table 3-5. (Chapter 5 discusses the incentives which the Japanese government provides for overseas minerals exploration.) In addition to these eleven projects, the Japanese government's Metal Mining Agency is supporting exploration work in the Ingessana Hills in Sudan in search of chromite deposits and in the Tessoum area of central Niger, where exploratory drilling for uranium deposits is under way.

In the petroleum field there are currently three Japanese projects in Black Africa. Two are in Gabon. The first, established in February 1972, involves the Mitsubishi Corp. and other Japanese partners, with

Table 3-4

SECTORAL DISTRIBUTION OF JAPANESE INVESTMENT
IN AFRICA, 1981[a]

Sector and Subsector	Number of Cases	Value (Millions of dollars)	Share in Total Japanese African Investment (Percent)	Share in Total Japanese FDI in Sector (Percent)
Manufacturing				
Food	29	$ 8	0.4%	1.1%
Textiles	48	38	1.9	2.2
Lumber and pulp	1	_b	_b	_b
Chemicals	8	16	0.8	0.6
Ferrous and nonferrous metals	23	75	3.7	2.4
Electrical machinery	6	5	0.2	0.2
Transport machinery	3	6	0.3	0.4
Other	8	6	0.3	0.6
Subtotal	126	154	7.6	1.0
Non-manufacturing				
Agriculture and forestry	12	7	0.4	1.0
Fisheries and marine	67	54	2.7	16.1
Mining	115	516	25.6	5.4
Construction	12	19	0.9	3.9
Commerce	20	3	0.2	0.1
Banking and insurance	11	2	0.1	0.1
Services	37	283	14.0	14.0
Transportation	43	199	9.9	27.6
Other	350	777	38.5	16.7
Subtotal	667	1860	92.2	6.5
Branch establishment and expansion	10	1	0.1	_b
Real estate	21	2	0.1	0.3
TOTAL	824	2018	100.0	4.4

Source: Same as Table 3-2.

[a]Includes North Africa.

[b]Negligible.

47

Table 3-5

JOINT VENTURES OF JAPANESE FIRMS IN MINERALS EXPLOITATION
IN AFRICA, 1981

Country	Mineral	Number of Japanese Joint Ventures
Gabon	Oil	2
Kenya	Fluorspar	1[a]
Liberia	Iron	1[b]
Niger	Uranium	2[c]
Senegal	Iron	1
Zaire	Copper	2
	Oil	1

Source: Document provided by MITI.

[a]Currently being phased out.

[b]At projection stage.

[c]One at projection stage.

50 percent of the equity being held by the SNEA. The total capital invested is 22.75 billion yen. The second project—the Gabon Oil Co. Ltd.—was initiated in March 1974. Two Japanese consortia—World Energy Development and C. Itoh Energy Development—are in partnership with ELF (30 percent shareholding) in an investment which totals 0.50 billion yen. The third petroleum project currently under way is in Zaire. It was established in August 1970 with Teikoku Oil in partnership with Muanda (Belgium) and Gulf, whose shareholdings in the 2.04 billion yen investment are 17.72 and 50 percent respectively. To date Japan has not been involved in petroleum production in Nigeria. An official of Mitsui, interviewed by us in Tokyo, stated that his company had lost interest in a joint venture in Nigeria as a result of changing Nigerian demands which would have made production unprofitable for the Japanese partner.* In total, Africa accounts

*In January 1983 we interviewed a substantial number of officials from major Japanese corporations, as well as government representatives, on issues relating to FDI. For brevity, we shall hereafter refer to these as the Tokyo interviews.

for 24 percent of Japan's overseas investments in the production of oil, 15 percent of its investments in iron ore production, and 24 percent of its investments in copper production.

Table 3-6 shows the principal Japanese overseas investments in Africa by country and firm. It is immediately obvious that few of the reasons cited above for the growth of Japan's FDI apply to its investments in Africa. For example, inexpensive local labor is seldom mentioned by the corporations as a reason for locating in Africa; more frequently reference is made to host government policies which make local production more profitable than supplying the market from overseas. Two principal investment objectives are listed: the procurement of raw materials and the gaining of royalties. None of the manufacturing concerns exports to Japan. Only one company (Mitsui & Co., based in Nigeria) mentions exports to third countries as one of its objectives. Apart from the Liberian-based shipping companies, most of the projects are joint ventures with fairly small capital.

THE ROLE OF TRADING COMPANIES IN FOREIGN INVESTMENT

Notable among the names of Japanese investors in Africa are the *sogo shosha*, the major trading companies. Mitsubishi, Marubeni, C. Itoh, Nichimen, Mitsui, and Sumitomo are prominent in a number of ventures, sometimes in association with smaller Japanese companies. The trading companies play a unique and significant role in Japanese foreign trade.

The origins of the trading companies date back to the 1870s, when Japan resumed international trade after more than two hundred years of self-imposed isolation. Major business interests set up specialized divisions or separate companies to provide the necessary expertise for pursuing new export opportunities, finding sources of raw materials and other imported products, and promoting industrial development in Japan. The need for specialized trading companies grew out of the contemporary ignorance of foreign market opportunities and the lack of knowledge of foreign languages.[3] Today there are more than 8,600 corporations in Japan classified as trading companies, although the largest 9 of these dominate the field (accounting for over 50 percent of Japan's total overseas trade). The discussion in this section will concentrate on these largest trading companies since they are the main Japanese actors in Africa.

49

Table 3-6

JAPANESE INVESTMENTS IN AFRICA BY COUNTRY AND FIRM, 1979[a]

African Country and Japanese Investor	Capital Ratio (Percent)	Names of Companies	Date of Operation Start	Capital[b]	Number of Employees	Major Business Lines	Annual Sales and/or Production	Partner Firms	Investment Reasons and Objectives[c]	Business Results	Location
ETHIOPIA											
Mitsubishi Corp.	100%	Mitsubishi Ethiopia Trading Private Ltd.		300,000		Trading		–			Addis Ababa
Mitsubishi Corp.	45	Ethio-Japan Auto Service Private Ltd.	12/72	500,000		Sales of automobile tires		E. Amalgamated (41%)[d] Mitsubishi Ethiopia Trading (5%)			Addis Ababa
Toray Industries Mitsubishi Corp. Sakai Textile Mfg.	32.45 13.95 3.6	Ethio-Japanese Synthetic Textiles Share Co.	9/66		530	Nylon fabrics; dyeing & finishing		Ministry of National Resources (50%)	C E	Paying dividends	Addis Ababa
Yokohama Rubber Mitsubishi Corp.	5.2 0.9	Addis Tyre Co., S.C.	10/72	2.87 mil.	600	Automobile tires & tubes	2,200 tons	Ministry of Industry (93.9%)	C I	Breaking even	Addis Ababa
KENYA											
Chori	100	Chori East Africa Co.	5/64	350,000		Imports of textile machinery, chemicals, steel raw materials		–	E F		Nairobi
Hirata Spinning	45	Kenya Fishnet Industries Ltd.	5/72	2 mil.	90	Fishing nets	60 tons; $800,000[f]	Industrial and Commercial Development Corp. (ICDC), Hon. W.O. Omamo (55%)	D G I		Kisumu
Iwatani & Co.	50	Iwatani-Lonata Vermiculite Co. of Kenya Ltd.	2/74	814,000	35	Development & imports of iron ores		Lonata Promotion Ltd. (50%)	A		Nairobi

Table 3-6 (cont.)

African Country and Japanese Investor	Capital Ratio (Percent)	Names of Companies	Date of Operation Start	Capital	Number of Employees	Major Business Lines	Annual Sales and/or Production	Partner Firms	Investment Reasons and Objectives	Business Results	Location
Sanyo Electric	48	African Radio Mfg. Co.	Capital participation in 1/73	4.4 mil.	240	Household electric appliances		ICDC, other (52%)	E	Paying dividends	Nairobi
Shikibo Nomura Trading[c]	24.54 / 24.54	United Textile Industry (Kenya)	2/64	8 mil.	700	Cotton print	KS26.46 mil.	Mar. Lakhamshi (50.92%)	C D I		Thika
LIBERIA											
Daiichi Chuo Kisen	100	Pacific Global Transport (Liberia) Inc.	1/76	1 mil.		Shipping	$1.69 mil.	-	E	Breaking even	Monrovia
Japan Line	100	Delphi Tankers Co.	12/71	10,000		Shipping		-			Monrovia
Japan Line	100	Erato Shipping Inc.	5/72	10,000		Shipping		-			Monrovia
Japan Line	100	Hillside Shipping Ltd.	10/75	1.7 mil.		Shipping, related business		-	C D		Monrovia
Japan Line	100	Northern Islanders Shipping Ltd.	10/76	5,000		Shipping, related business		-	C D		Monrovia
Japan Line	100	Bayard Tanker Corp.	1977	9,300		Shipping, related business		-	C D		Monrovia
Japan Line	100	Southern Islanders Shipping Ltd.	7/77	5,000		Shipping, related business		-	C D		Monrovia
Kawasaki Kisen	100	Luna Navigation Co.	Absorbed in 9/77	700,000		Shipping	$2.62 mil.	-	C G H		Monrovia
Kawasaki Kisen	100	Diamond River Co.	4/72	500		Shipping		-			Monrovia
Kawasaki Kisen	40	Pan Asia Tanker Services Inc.	5/73	6,250		Shipping		Island Navigation (60%)			Monrovia
Kawasaki Kisen / C. Itoh & Co.	34 / 33	Univenture Shipping Corp.	7/73	50,000		Shipping		Motorships (33%)	G		Monrovia
Kawasaki Kisen	100	Rioship Co.	8/73	2.4 mil.		Shipping		-			Monrovia

Table 3-6 (cont.)

African Country and Japanese Investor	Capital Ratio (*Percent*)	Names of Companies	Date of Operation Start	Capital	Number of Employees	Major Business Lines	Annual Sales and/or Production	Partner Firms	Investment Reasons and Objectives	Business Results	Location
Kawasaki Kisen	50	Gemini Maritime Corp.	6/74	1 mil.		Shipping		Intermarine Maritime Corp. (50%)	C		Monrovia
Kawasaki Kisen	100	Argus Shipping Co.	10/77	1,000		Shipping		-	G H		Monrovia
Kawasaki Steel Corp. Nissho Iwai Corp. Toyo Menka Kaisha Marubeni Corp. C. Itoh & Co.	30.8	Liberia Iron & Steel Corp.	Planned	20.48 mil.	100	Mining		Amax, LIAC, other[g] (69.2%)	A		Monrovia
Mitsui & Co.	100	Lepta Shipping Co.	4/74	3 mil.		Shipping		-			Monrovia
Mitsui & Co.	100	Graciela Shipping Co.	12/78	1,000		Shipping		-			Monrovia
Mitsui & Co.	100	Bright Shipping Inc.	4/79	10,000		Shipping		-			Monrovia
Mitsui & Co. Kanbara Kisen	50 50	Tri-Ever Shipping Ltd.	5/78	2.8 mil.		Shipping		-			Monrovia
Sanko Steamship Toyo Menka Kaisha	50 50	Green Shipping & Trading S.A.	11/76	4.4 mil.		Shipping		-			Monrovia
Sanko Steamship Toyo Menka Kaisha	50 50	Santo Shipping & Trading S.A.	4/76	4.4 mil.		Shipholding, leasing of ships		-			Monrovia
Shinwa Kaiun	20	Liberian Angel Transports Inc.	5/73	1.5 mil.		Loans		-			Monrovia
Nippon Suisan	100	Excellent Steamship Co.	2/75	1.6 mil.		Shipping	$280,000	-	C	Breaking even	Monrovia
Showa Line	100	Vivid Transport Inc., Liberia	9/79	2,000		Shipholding, leasing of ships		-	G H	Breaking even	Monrovia
Showa Line	50	Septa Shipping Ltd.	12/74	5,000		Shipping		Fairmont Enterprise (50%)			Monrovia
Showa Line	50	Continental Bulk-carriers Inc.	4/74	5,000		Shipping		Maritime Foundation (50%)			Monrovia

Table 3-6 (cont.)

African Country and Japanese Investor	Capital Ratio (Percent)	Names of Companies	Date of Operation Start	Capital	Number of Employees	Major Business Lines	Annual Sales and/or Production	Partner Firms	Investment Reasons and Objectives	Business Results	Location
Showa Line	50	Octa Shipping Ltd.	2/75	5,000		Shipping		Fairmont Enterprise (50%)			Monrovia
Showa Line	100	Alioth Transport Inc.	11/76	10,000		Shipping					Monrovia
Showa Line	50	Liberian Sonia Transports Inc.	3/76	5,000		Shipping		Liberian Raffia Transport (50%)			Monrovia
Showa Line	100	Liberian Coral Transports Inc.	3/76	500		Shipping; subsidiary of Liberian Sonia Transports		-			Monrovia
Showa Line	100	Liberian Ivory Transports Inc.	3/76	500		Shipping		-			Monrovia
Showa Line	100	Benetnasch Transport Inc.	7/76	10,000		Shipping		-			Monrovia
Showa Line	100	Dubhe Transport Inc., Liberia	12/77	2.31 mil.		Shipping		-			Monrovia
Showa Line	100	Lucid Shipping Inc.	10/77	1,000		Shipping		-			Monrovia
Showa Line	100	Sun Shipping (Liberia) Inc.	12/78	500		Shipholding, leasing of ships	$2 mil.	-	G H	Breaking even	Monrovia
Showa Line	100	Taharoa Maritime Inc., Liberia	3/78	10,000		Shipping		-			Monrovia
Taiheiyo Kaiun	100	Carina Navigation Corp.	3/77	1,000		Shipping	$2.56 mil.	-	E	No dividends	Monrovia
Taiheiyo Kaiun	66.7	Oceanhope Shipping Co.	4/78	3,000		Shipping	$3.8 mil.	Hop Chung Shipping Co. (33.3%)	E	No dividends	Monrovia
Taiyo Fishery	100	East Atalntic Ltd.	1973	5.3 mil.		Shipping		-			Monrovia
Taiyo Fishery	100	New Eastern Ltd.	1975	3.2 mil.		Shipping		-			Monrovia
Tamai Shosen	100	T.S. Central Shipping Co.	1975	1,000		Shipping	$2.41 mil.	-	G H	Deficit	Monrovia

Table 3-6 (cont.)

African Country and Japanese Investor	Capital Ratio (Percent)	Names of Companies	Date of Operation Start	Capital	Number of Employees	Major Business Lines	Annual Sales and/or Production	Partner Firms	Investment Reasons and Objectives	Business Results	Location
Toyo Menka Kaisha	15	Strait Shipping & Trading Inc.	8/78	6.5 mil.		Shipping		Demeter Shipping Co. (85%)			Monrovia
Yamashita-Shinnihon Steamship	100	Valiant Shipping Co.	5/71	50,000		Shipping		-	C	No dividends	Monrovia
Yamashita-Shinnihon Steamship	100	Hoover Shipping Co.	5/71	50,000		Shipping		-	C	No dividends	Monrovia
Yamashita-Shinnihon Steamship	100	Sunny Shipping Co.	6/71	120,000		Shipping		-	C	No dividends	Monrovia
Yamashita-Shinnihon Steamship	100	Liberian Panda Transports Inc.	1978	500		Shipping		-	C	No dividends	Monrovia
NIGERIA											
C. Itoh & Co.	40	C. Itoh & Co. (Nigeria) Ltd.	10/78	2,400		Data collection, other activities		Chief Thomas (30%), other (30%)	F		Lagos
C. Itoh & Co. Yodogawa Steel Works	24 / 12	Galvanizing Industries Ltd.	5/64	2.5 mil.	504	Production of galvanized iron sheets		Compagnie Française Africaine Occidentale (CFAO), other (64%)			Lagos
Daiwa Spinning Chori	5.3 / 5.3	Bhojsons Industries Ltd.	11/70	4.28 mil.	670	Woven cloths; dyeing & processing	$23.6 mil.;[f] 840 yards	Local capital (89.4%)	E	Paying dividends	Lagos
Hirata Spinning Asahi Chemical Ind. C. Itoh & Co.	22.5 / 19.4 / 19.4	Ninetco Ltd.	9/71	1.2 mil.	492	Processing of nylon fishing nets		CFAO (38.75%)	G R		Lagos
Honda Motor			Planned			Production of motorcycles		Local capital	E I		Lagos
Kuraray Marubeni Corp.	11 / 6	Woollen & Synthetic Textile Mfg. Ltd.	Capital participation in 3/70	800,000	319	Woven cloths, knitted goods	N£5 mil.	National Investment Development Board (NIDB) (20%), J.T. Chanrai, other (63%)	G I	Paying dividends	Lagos

Table 3-6 (cont.)

African Country and Japanese Investor	Capital Ratio (Percent)	Names of Companies	Date of Operation Start	Capital	Number of Employees	Major Business Lines	Annual Sales and/or Production	Partner Firms	Investment Reasons and Objectives	Business Results	Location
Mitsubishi Corp. Kobe Steel	17.3 10.2	Standard Industrial Development Co.	7/77	1 mil.		Small-caliber steel tubes, light section steel		John Holt Nigerian Pension Scheme, other (72.5%)	E I		Lagos
Mitsui & Co.	30	Nigerian Wire Industries Ltd.	11/73	2.5 mil.	700	Production of steel rod secondary products		Bridon Ltd., other (70%)	E J		Lagos
Nichimen	20	Metcome Nigeria Ltd.	1/77	1 mil.	63	Processing & sales of steel products	N£9.48 mil.	J.R. Anyachie & Co. (40%), other (40%)	C E I	Paying dividends	Aba
Nippon Kokan Marubeni Corp. G.H. Kato & Co.	19.1 19.1 1.3	Pioneer Metal Products Co.	6/64	3.12 mil.	540	Galvanized iron sheets	60,000 tons; N£19 mil.	Paterson Zochonis, G.H. Elice, other (60.5%)	D E I	Paying dividends	Lagos
Sanyo Electric Marubeni Corp.	15 15	Sanyo Nigeria Ltd.	2/69	800,000	350	Assembly & sales of home electric appliances		A.G. Leventis, individual investors (70%)	E		Ibadan
Sekisui Chemical Nichimen	30 10	Eslon Nigeria Ltd.	1977	600,000		Polyvinyl chloride pipes, polyethylene films		NNIL (30%), NRDL, other (30%)	E I		Kaduna
Sumitomo Corp.	40	Sumitomo Shoji Kaisha (Nigeria) Ltd.	12/78	10,000	11	Marketing surveying, data collection		Local capital (60%)	F		Lagos
Sumitomo Electric Ind. Sumitomo Corp.	40 20	Nigerian Wire & Cable Co.	4/78	2.8 mil.	245	Electric wires & cables		Odu'a Investment Co. (40%)	I		Ibadan
Taiyo Fishery	30	Osadjere Fishing Co.	9/74	1 mil.	382	Prawn trawling; processing, freezing, & sales of marine products		Ibru Seafood Ltd. (70%)	A		Lagos
Teijin C. Itoh & Co.	25 25	Nigeria Teijin Textiles Ltd.	4/71	3.1 mil.	1,055	Spinning, weaving, dyeing, & processing of Tetoron, rayon	$12.94 mil.f	CFAO Nigeria Ltd. (50%)	C D I	Paying dividends	Lagos

Table 3-6 (cont.)

African Country and Japanese Investor	Capital Ratio (Percent)	Names of Companies	Date of Operation Start	Capital	Number of Employees	Major Business Lines	Annual Sales and/or Production	Partner Firms	Investment Reasons and Objectives	Business Results	Location
Toray Industries	19.3	General Cotton Mill Ltd.	Capital participation in 9/73	8.4 mil.	2,950	Spinning & weaving of polyester/cotton mixed fabrics	$40 mil.[f]	Startex, other (80.7%)	C D	Paying dividends	Lagos
Toyobo & 8 other spinners	44.9	Arewa Textiles Ltd.	4/65	8.02 mil.	3,500	Dyeing, spinning, weaving, & processing	$2.0 mil.[f]	Local capital (40%), U.S., British firms (15.1%)	F		Lagos
Unitika / Nichimen	26 / 25	Zaria Industries Ltd.	4/75	1.96 mil.	489	Spinning, weaving, processing, & sales of canvas	$3.8 mil.[f]	Kaduna Investment Co., Industrial Development Bank (49%)	C D I		Kaduna
ZAIRE											
Japan Steel Works 52 / Furukawa Mining 9 / Mitsubishi Metal 6 / Nissho-Iwai 5 / Dowa Mining 4		Société de Dévelopement Industriel et Minier du Zaire	10/72	$6 mil.[f]	2,458	Copper mining		Zaire government (15%)	A		Lumumbashi
Long-Term Credit Bank of Japan 0.625 / Bank of Tokyo 0.625 / Industrial Bank of Japan 0.625		Société Financière de Dévelopement	Capital participation in 6/70	4 mil.		Medium- & long-term loans		International Finance Corporation (IFC) (17.75%), local government, local banks, other (80.375%)			Kinshasa
Marubeni Corp.	16	Société Minière de Moba	Planned	250,000		Development of copper mines		SEREM (32%), SOGEREM (16%), SNPA (16%), Zaire government (20%)	A		Kinshasa
Mitsui & Co.	14	Société Minière de Tenke-Fungurume	1/71	2 mil.	850	Non-ferrous metal ores & other natural resources development		Zaire government, other (86%)	A		Kinshasa

Table 3-6 (cont.)

African Country and Japanese Investor	Capital Ratio (Percent)	Names of Companies	Date of Operation Start	Capital	Number of Employees	Major Business Lines	Annual Sales and/or Production	Partner Firms	Investment Reasons and Objectives	Business Results	Location
Mitsui & Co.	14	Société Internationale des Mines du Zaire	1/72	2 mil.		Non-ferrous metal ores & other natural resources development		Zaire government, other (86%)	A		Kinshasa
Mitsui Bank	10	CITI Bank (Zaire) SARL	Capital participation in 4/74	250,000	60	General banking		Local capital (90%)			Kinshasa
Nichimen	18	C.P.A. Zaire SARL	Capital participation in 11/72	4.37 mil.	1,010	Dyeing & processing	Z30 mil.	Tootal (30%), Gamma Holding (20%), SIMIS (22.5%), local government (9.5%)	R		Kinshasa
Yodogawa Steel Works / C. Itoh & Co.	10 / 10	Société de Galvanisation de Kinshasa	2/71	600,000	106	Galvanized iron sheets		Mr. Rawji, other (80%)	D	Paying dividends	Kinshasa

Source: Adapted from *Oriental Economist* (Tokyo), October 1980: 38-43.

[a]The information in this table is from a survey of May 1979 by *Oriental Economist*. The survey is based primarily on questionnaires (as well as telephone calls and other methods of inquiry) to leading Japanese corporations, both listed on the nation's stock exchanges—mostly in Tokyo, Osaka, and Nagoya—and unlisted companies which have joint investments with listed companies. Investment cases were eliminated when unlisted companies had greater investment shares than their listed partners.

[b]Unless otherwise indicated, capital is expressed in the currency of the host country, as follows: Ethiopia–Ethiopian Birr; Kenya–Kenya shillings (KS); Liberia–U.S. dollars; Nigeria–Nigerian pounds (N£); Zaire–Zaires (Z).

[c]Investment reasons and objectives are identified as follows: A–Procurement of raw materials; B–Easy local production due to abundant natural resources; C–Utilization of inexpensive labor and reduction of costs; D–More profitable local production due to industrial promotion and protection policies by domestic governments; E–Expansion of sales to local and third-country markets; F–Data collection; G–Other purposes; H–Exports to Japan; I–Local market; J–Exports to third countries; R–Gaining of royalties.

[d]Figures in parentheses represent partner's share of equity.

[e]Unlisted companies are identified in italics.

[f]Figure in U.S. dollars.

[g]Where company acronyms are not identified, the company is known in the host country only by its acronym.

The basic role of the trading companies is in marketing and distribution—they are trading rather than manufacturing conglomerates. They maintain representative offices in the principal cities around the world. (A list of their African offices is provided in Table 3-7.) These offices are responsible for collecting business information of all kinds. The companies' knowledge of trading opportunities provides them with an advantage over individual manufacturers marketing their own products—especially since they specialize in piecing together package deals involving a number of companies and products. Recently their business has expanded to encompass third-country trade—i.e., the promotion of trade between two foreign countries without Japanese involvement as a source of supply or as a market. In addition to marketing, the trading companies arrange for the transportation, insurance, and warehousing of the products they trade.[4]

The trading firms have a business strategy based on a long-term perspective. They are accustomed and prepared to make substantial investments in research and investigation of prospects for new products and (in some cases) emerging new industries overseas and at home. Often they work closely in pursuing their objectives with the Ministry of International Trade and Industry (MITI) and other government agencies in a somewhat symbiotic relationship. Trading companies also play several other important international roles. For example, they serve as financial intermediaries by borrowing big and lending small. Using the borrowing power derived from the sheer scale of its operations, a trading company can obtain money from the major Japanese banks at relatively low interest rates and lend these funds to the small businesses with which it deals. The loans are generally tied to specific uses and often take the form of providing imported raw materials on credit and financing new construction or prepayments on export sales. In 1974 the six largest sogo shosha alone accounted for 34 percent of the total commercial credit extended by Japan's major corporations.[5]

Another important function of the trading companies in the financing area is their ability to absorb foreign exchange risks for their customers. Given their large size, the sogo shosha are in a position to make commitments to buy products from a Japanese producer in yen even though the export sales contract may be in dollars or another foreign currency. They are able to do this on a large scale because they handle both export and import transactions and can thus internally

Table 3-7

OFFICES OF JAPANESE TRADING FIRMS ON AFRICAN CONTINENT

Location of Office	Trading Company					
	Mitsubishi	Mitsui	Marubeni	Kanematsu Gosho	C. Itoh	Sumitomo
Type of Office[a]						
Abidjan	X	X	X	—	X	X
Accra	—	—	X	—	X	—
Addis Ababa	XX	X	X	—	X	—
Dakar	—	—	—	X	—	—
Dar es Salaam	X	X	X	—	X	X
Douala	XX	X	X	—	XX	—
Harare	X	X	—	—	X	X
Johannes- burg	X	XX	XX	X	XX	XX
Khartoum	X	X	X	X	—	—
Kinshasa	X	X	—	—	X	X
Kitwe	X	X	—	—	—	—
Lagos	XX	XX	XX	—	X	X
Libreville	—	—	—	—	X	—
Luanda	—	X	—	—	X	X
Lusaka	X	X	X	—	X	X
Maputo	—	—	—	—	—	X
Nairobi	X	X	XX	—	X	X
Yaoundé	—	XX	—	—	—	—

Source: Information supplied by U.S. Embassy, Tokyo.

[a]The types of offices are as follows: X—representative office; XX—branch or local subsidiary office.

offset exchange losses with gains. Absorbing exchange rate losses has been a particularly valuable service in recent years as exchange rates have tended to fluctuate considerably under the present floating rate regime.

In addition, the trading companies have an important role in the FDI activities of Japanese companies and in investment by foreigners in Japan. Given their access to overseas information and their business connections in other countries, they are in a good position to find profitable investment possibilities for Japanese firms and arrange joint ventures with local participants. Smaller Japanese firms tend to rely on the trading companies to assist them in setting up investments abroad. (Larger manufacturing firms, on the other hand, are generally able to make overseas investments on their own.) The trading companies are typically important to foreigners because of their participation in Japanese distribution channels and their knowledge of Japanese firms. They also often participate in joint marketing ventures with foreign partners.

The advantages of the trading companies in arranging large-scale integrated resource projects are obvious: they are able to piece together packages of equipment, technology, and consulting services from numerous manufacturers—not merely from Japan but from all available sources. Even in Africa, where the prospects for intra-African trade are somewhat daunting, the trading companies are playing a pioneering role: Mitsui, which manufactures bottles for Coca-Cola in Nigeria, purchases the caustic soda needed in the glass-making process from Kenya.

JAPANESE PERCEPTIONS OF THE AFRICAN INVESTMENT ENVIRONMENT

Despite their relative success in increasing their investments in Africa in recent years, Japanese businesses generally regard the investment climate there with the same feelings as their Western competitors. In a survey of Japanese businesses operating in Africa, the problem mentioned most frequently was political instability.[6] (In other regions instability was listed sixth in the problems cited.) Other problems frequently mentioned—in order of perceived importance—were the difficulties of raising capital, the quality of labor, economic instability, and the difficulties of collecting information. The companies surveyed noted that investment in Africa involved more problems that could not be solved by their own efforts than did investment in any other region of the world.

Although Japanese companies have had some success in penetrating Francophone Africa, Japanese investors complained of the difficulties that they experienced not only as a result of language barriers, but also because of the continuing French presence in many of these countries. A number of the officials quoted in Chiyoura Masamichi's study perceived a tendency on the part of some African countries to automatically give preference to EC commercial interests. Moreover, many African countries had adopted European industrial standards. Japanese investors also noted that they had experienced difficulty in understanding African cultures and believed that they were disliked in some parts of Africa for being one-dimensional "economic animals." Although willing to participate in joint ventures, Japanese investors were generally wary of demands for increased African participation in shareholding, management, and intermediate inputs. One trading company official recounted to us how his company—involved in the production of galvanized roofing sheets—had been able to resist further Africanization because its parent company was the sole source of the specialized steel needed for this production.

In general, in our Tokyo interviews, officials of both the public and private sectors were pessimistic regarding future Japanese investments in Africa. They perceived little scope for expanding import-substituting manufacturing owing to the economic crisis afflicting most African countries. Furthermore, they had lost their enthusiasm for minerals investments in Africa. Many spoke of the mounting frustrations with political instability and with the problems of transporting raw materials to ports once they had been extracted. Zaire in particular was singled out for criticism, with a number of trading companies' representatives noting that they planned no further involvement in that country. While Japan continues to seek to diversify its sources of raw materials, the urgency and anxiety which existed immediately after a successful oil embargo in 1973-74 by the Organization of Petroleum Exporting Countries (OPEC) have disappeared. Japan's principal concern at present is to establish secure sources of supply, a dimension on which Africa is not perceived to score highly.[7] This is reflected in the decline in Japanese investment in Niger, Nigeria, and Zaire since the mid-1970s (see Table 3-3).

EMERGING JAPANESE ECONOMIC INFLUENCE IN AFRICA

JAPAN AND SOUTH AFRICA[8]

Since 1968 the Japanese government has prohibited Japanese companies from engaging in direct investment in the Republic of South Africa. This ban, however, has not prevented Japanese companies from playing a major role in the economic development of the Republic.

Japanese commercial relations with South Africa expanded rapidly in the early 1960s. Following the Sharpeville Massacre (1960)* and the subsequent exodus of foreign capital, the South African government desperately sought to encourage new sources of foreign investment. As part of this move, the Japanese were granted "honorary white" status in the Republic in 1961. During the 1960s trade between South Africa and Japan grew in value by over 500 percent. However, it was in the 1970s that Japanese penetration of the South African economy increased dramatically, despite Japan's prohibition on direct investment. In 1971 all of the major trading companies established branch offices in South Africa, and in the early 1970s a large number of local subsidiaries of Japanese manufacturing companies were also established.

Toyota had been a pioneer in South Africa. Its first assembly plant was established in 1962. In 1971 its operations were moved to a new plant on the border of one of the homelands to take advantage of tax incentives. The new plant, which produces 85 percent of Toyota vehicles sold in South Africa (the company's third largest market), is the company's largest assembly plant outside Japan. Toyota was followed into the South African market by the other principal Japanese car manufacturers (Nissan, Mitsubishi, Isuzu, and Toyo Kogyo [Mazda]), Japanese tire companies (Bridgestone, Yokohama, and Toyo Rubber), motorcycle manufacturers (Honda, Yamaha, and Suzuki), and manufacturers of electronic and electrical appliances (Matsushita, Hitachi, Sanyo, Sony, Sharp, Sansui, Pioneer, and Akai— among others). In most cases these subsidiaries are wholly locally owned with capital raised from South African banks; they hold a franchise from the Japanese parent for the production of the corporation's range of goods.

*Police shot demonstrators protesting a requirement that Blacks carry passbooks.

Some corporations have been able to circumvent the ban on direct investment of Japanese capital by investing through their overseas subsidiaries and affiliates; there have also been instances of South African subsidiaries of European companies raising capital in Japan for investment in South Africa.[9] However, one of the two major contributions of Japanese corporations to South African economic development has not come through the investment of capital but through the transfer of patents, technology, and management skills (for example) to their locally franchised partners. This type of transfer offers a number of benefits to the Japanese parent corporations: not only do they reap financial rewards from licenses and from the sale of components and management skills, but also the fact that the companies are owned by South Africans and run by South African managers insulates the Japanese corporations from criticism regarding local labor conditions and disputes, as well as the operations of the apartheid system. These local subsidiaries are entirely free from Japanese government controls and pressures.

Japan's other major contribution to South Africa's economic development has come from its guaranteeing a long-term market for exports of some of the Republic's minerals. In the early 1970s Japan's iron and steel industry looked to South Africa as a means of reducing its dependence on Australian ores; the South Africans, meanwhile, saw the exploitation of iron ore deposits as a means of diversifying their exports and of improving infrastructure. Thus was born a marriage of convenience. In July 1971 the principal corporations in the Japanese iron and steel industry even went so far as to petition their government (unsuccessfully) to lift the ban on direct investment to South Africa.[10] Even without direct investment participation from Japan, the ten to fifteen year contracts signed by Japanese corporations provided the necessary security for large-scale mineral projects to go ahead. Some of the more important were the opening of new mines at Sishen and the associated improvement of port facilities at Saldanha Bay and St. Croix. Similar long-term contracts in the coal industry have facilitated the construction of a new rail system in Natal linking up with a major port development at Richard Bay.

Japanese corporations have benefited not only from secure sources of supply, but also from contracts for plant and machinery arising from the expansion of the South African steel industry which has accompanied the opening up of new iron mines. Undoubtedly there has been an element of reciprocity in the transactions. In announcing the award of a contract for an oxygen furnace to Mitsui—reportedly the single most valuable machinery contract ever given by the Republic—South Africa explained that Mitsui had won the award because it had been the principal agent in arranging an important Japan-South Africa coal deal.[11] Similarly Mitsubishi won a $33 million order in 1971 from South Africa's Iron and Steel Corporation for the construction of a semi-continuous steel rolling mill. This was the largest single order received by the company in the early 1970s and amounted to 15 percent of its yearly exports. The contract was signed on the basis of deferred-payment financing provided by Japan's Export-Import (EXIM) Bank.[12]

Aside from iron and coal, Japan has shown particular interest in South African uranium. Japan's ambitious plans for reducing its dependency on imported oil by promoting nuclear energy have necessitated a dramatic increase in imports of uranium. By December 1973 Japan's power companies had already signed long-term contracts covering 80 percent of the estimated uranium import needs for the ten-year period beginning in 1975. South Africa (including Namibia) is the single most important source, supplying 43 percent of total uranium imports. Japan's long-term purchase contract from the RTZ-Rossing mine in Namibia violated UN resolutions on trade with that territory. As in the case of iron, Japan has supplied equipment to help South Africa with the processing of uranium ore—in this case the South African uranium-enrichment plant.

Chapter 4

JAPANESE OVERSEAS DEVELOPMENT ASSISTANCE

POLICY AND ADMINISTRATION OF FOREIGN CAPITAL TRANSFERS

Japanese overseas transfers in the post-World War II period initially took the form of technical assistance to Asian neighbors as part of international technical cooperation schemes such as the UN Expanded Program of Technical Assistance and the Colombo Plan. Later a number of reparations agreements were signed—with Burma in 1955, the Philippines in 1956, and Indonesia in 1958—while grants in lieu of formal reparations were arranged with Laos and Cambodia in 1959. These served both to meet international commitments and to promote the exports of industries established as part of postwar reconstruction. The first yen loan, a contribution to the World Bank Consortium for India, was made in 1958. It was followed by other loans to Paraguay, South Vietnam, Pakistan, and Brazil, but the sums involved were small: the volume of net official flows actually fell in the years 1958-61.[1]

In this early period no attempt was made to distinguish aid from other types of public and private overseas economic relations (e.g., export credits); all were grouped under the heading of "economic cooperation." A 1958 report from MITI stated that economic cooperation could refer to relations not only between developed and developing countries, but also to those between Japan and other developed countries. There was no reference in this report to "aid" as such. To further add to the confusion, the various ministries concerned with overseas economic relations—primarily the Ministry of Foreign Affairs, MITI, the Ministry of Finance, and the Economic Planning Agency—drew up their own priorities for economic cooperation with no agency having the responsibility of coordinating the various policies.

There was a consensus, however, regarding the purposes that economic cooperation should serve. It was expressed clearly in a 1961

65

MITI report: Japan undertook economic cooperation not for political objectives arising from the Cold War, nor as support for developmental objectives resulting from decolonization, but in order to develop domestic industry. MITI repeatedly emphasized in the 1960s that economic cooperation was part of an overall trade policy whose intention was to benefit the Japanese economy. Emphasis by the Japanese government on the trade effects of aid brought considerable criticism from Third World representatives.* However, the theme of promoting economic cooperation for domestic benefit has until recently remained prominent in the Japanese approach to aid. When the Japan International Cooperation Agency was established in 1973, Prime Minister Kakuei Tanaka announced that its purpose was to develop resources for Japan's benefit; accordingly its activities would not be restricted to developing countries but would include other potentially important sources of raw materials—e.g., Australia. In the past five years there has been a change in emphasis by the Japanese government: priority in recent official reports has been given to themes such as growing interdependence, basic human needs, and security interests of the Western alliance.

One reason for the historic emphasis on domestic interests has been the need to attempt to "sell" foreign aid to the Japanese public. Neither within the government nor the public is there widespread support for foreign aid; there is no effective aid lobby such as that found in other member countries of the Organization for Economic Cooperation and Development (OECD). A noted Japanese sociologist, Chie Nakane, attributes the general attitude toward aid to the Confucian ethic of the Japanese population and to the absence of any sense of *noblesse oblige*.[2] This is one reason behind the small contribution to overseas development made by Japanese private voluntary agencies; in recent years they have contributed only slightly over 1 percent of the total grants by private agencies from OECD countries. It also helps to explain the low grant content of Japanese aid until 1980. The belief was widespread among officials that grant aid was neither economically nor psychologically sound since it placed recipients in the position of gaining something for nothing. Especially in the early years of Japan's aid program an emphasis in the evaluation

---

*For example, criticism came at the first meeting of the United Nations Conference on Trade and Development in 1964—known as UNCTAD I.

of aid requests was placed on countries which were perceived to be willing to help themselves. No capital grants were made until 1969. When they were introduced, they were extended to middle-income developing countries which enjoyed "friendly relations" with Japan, although in principle capital grants were supposed to be confined to the least developed countries.

In the absence of a strong domestic constituency the funding of economic cooperation was more than usually vulnerable to sacrifice in times of budgetary stringency. A number of observers have noted the important role of the budgetary process in Japan in making policy. Since there was no single bureaucratic "home" to defend the economic cooperation budget, it tended to receive low priority when matched against considerations of balance of payments and foreign exchange reserves. Accordingly the ratio of Japanese aid to GNP has fluctuated erratically, falling back at times when the economy experienced temporary balance-of-payments difficulties (e.g., in the mid-1970s).

According to Alan Rix, eleven ministries, three agencies, and the Prime Minister's Office have authority over various aspects of Japan's foreign aid program. Unlike the practice in most other OECD countries, there is no central aid agency and no single minister responsible for aid. Three ministries and one agency within the government share a major role in formulating economic cooperation policies: the Ministry of Finance, the Ministry of Foreign Affairs (MOFA), MITI, and the Economic Planning Agency. The latter administers the Overseas Economic Cooperation Fund, the leading organization in Japan's aid program, originally established as the Asian Development Fund within the EXIM Bank but made a separate agency in 1960.[3] Among the groups that decide aid policies, MOFA plays the key coordinating role.

Lack of a strong central aid agency and a shortage of staff within the ministries has made it very difficult for the Japanese government to undertake country programming of aid: most aid decisions are made on a case-by-case basis. Officially aid policy is passive: aid can be initiated only at the request of a potential recipient. Not surprisingly, this has made it difficult to achieve more than incremental change in the distribution of foreign aid. In many cases—particularly those involving large natural resource projects—the initiative in requesting aid is taken by private Japanese corporations which have an interest in promoting a particular project. Private firms often approach the government of the developing country and help it prepare and present a formal request in Tokyo. Aid officials noted that this has often been the case in Africa, where the small number of government representatives in the field leads to a heavy reliance on the private sector. The whole aid procedure is complicated by a budgetary process which in principle requires that projects be completed in the same fiscal year as a grant is voted and an exchange of notes with the potential recipient takes place. Any carryover of monies to the next fiscal year requires sanction by the Diet.

FOREIGN AID RECORD

As noted, Japan's aid effort in the past was frequently criticized by developing countries and aid professionals. Typical are the comments of John White, who characterized Japanese aid as "inadequate, wrongly motivated and administered, too narrowly and selectively applied, and out of line with the aid programmes of other donors."[4] Japan's ratio of Overseas Development Aid (ODA) to GNP has consistently lagged well behind the average of the OECD's Development Assistance Committee (DAC)—see Table 4-1. (It is interesting to note in this context that Japan joined the predecessor of the DAC prior to becoming a member of the OECD itself—but only after it had satisfied itself that the DAC would not be able to bind members to specific aid commitments.) Official Japanese publications have defended the aid record on a number of grounds: the absence of a colonial experience (which not only is perceived as relieving Japan of some of the responsibility for promoting development in the Third World, but also as handicapping the Japanese aid effort because the government lacked the familiarity that the former colonial powers enjoyed regarding their former colonies); a lack of experience in aid-giving; and urgent domestic demands on scarce resources. Initially the domestic factors were listed as balance-of-payments problems and a need for increased social expenditures. In recent years as the balance-of-payments constraint has largely disappeared, emphasis has been placed on the difficulties caused by persistent budgetary deficits.

Japan's unmatched record of sustained economic growth in the postwar era and its emergence as the second largest economy in the non-Communist world undermined the credibility of its excuses, particularly in the eyes of Third World leaders. Increasingly there has been a realization on the part of the Japanese government that its poor record on foreign aid was potentially harmful to its relations with the developing world, on which it was becoming ever more dependent for raw materials and for markets for its manufactured exports. OPEC's successful actions in 1973-74 were a shock which galvanized the government into a policy change. There were four principal dimensions to the shift in policy:

(1) *Quantitative*: a significant increase in flows. This policy goal was not realized until the late 1970s, however. The ODA/GNP ratio actually fell from 1974 to 1978, in part reflecting the problems experienced by the Japanese economy in the post-OPEC slump.

(2) *Qualitative*: an increase in the grant element in Japanese aid (in part necessitated by the new types of projects undertaken, as described below) and the untying of most aid. The latter was facilitated by the increasing competitiveness of Japanese industry; policymakers were confident that a large percentage of the contracts generated by untied aid would be awarded to Japanese corporations. Less than 1 percent of Japanese aid was untied in respect of all possible sources of supply in the mid-1970s. In 1977 untied loans were only 7 percent of the total; a further 76 percent were untied in favor of developing country procurement. In 1978 a commitment was made to the principle of untying all development loans. By 1980 untied aid in respect of all possible sources of supply had risen to over 65 percent. That year for the first time, all other aid was untied with reference to LDC sources. By 1981 58 percent of all new loan commitments were fully untied, and the remainder were untied in favor of procurement in developing countries.

(3) *Sectoral*: a move toward large-scale, integrated projects designed to develop overseas sources of raw materials and foodstuffs for export to Japan. The government played an active role in piecing together large aid packages with the Japanese private sector and the governments of potential beneficiaries. Increased support was given for feasibility studies, and new arrangements for export insurance made for corporations participating in the projects. The scale of the projects and the urgency with which

Table 4-1

FLOW OF FINANCIAL RESOURCES FROM JAPAN TO DEVELOPING COUNTRIES
AND MULTILATERAL AGENCIES, 1960-81

(Millions of dollars)

Financial Flow	1960	1961	1962	1963	1964	1965	1966	1967	1968	1969	1970	1971
Total official and private, net	$246.0	$381.4	$285.8	$278.4	$303.8	$485.5	$538.8	$855.3	$1029.8	$1263.1	$1823.9	$2140.5
ODA,[a] net	145.0	221.4	167.8	140.4	115.7	243.7	285.3	390.6	356.2	435.6	458.0	510.7
Bilateral	115.0	210.0	160.6	128.2	106.2	226.3	234.7	345.9	308.3	339.7	371.5	432.0
Grants	67.0	67.8	74.6	76.7	68.7	82.2	104.7	138.4	117.0	123.4	121.2	125.4
Loans	48.0	142.2	86.0	51.5	37.5	144.1	130.0	207.5	191.3	216.2	250.3	306.6
Multilateral	30.0	11.4	7.2	12.2	9.5	17.4	50.7	44.7	47.9	95.9	86.5	78.7
Other official flows, net[b]	N.A.	N.A.	82.9	35.9	94.9	109.7	182.7	198.9	322.1	375.8	693.6	651.1
Private, at market terms	101.0	160.0	118.0	138.0	188.1	241.8	253.5	464.7	351.5	541.7	669.4	975.6
Total/GNP *(Percent)*	0.57	0.71	0.49	0.40	0.36	0.55	0.62	0.67	0.73	0.76	0.93	0.92
DAC[c] average *(Percent)*	0.89	0.95	0.80	0.76	0.79	0.77	0.71	0.74	0.80	0.75	0.74	0.74
ODA/GNP *(Percent)*	0.24	0.20	0.15	0.20	0.15	0.28	0.28	0.32	0.25	0.26	0.23	0.23
DAC average *(Percent)*	0.52	0.53	0.52	0.51	0.49	0.44	0.41	0.42	0.38	0.36	0.34	0.35

Table 4-1 (cont.)

Financial Flow	1972	1973	1974	1975	1976	1977	1978	1979	1980	1981
Total official and private, net	$2725.4	$5844.2	$2962.3	$2879.6	$4002.6	$5534.9	$10703.5	$7555.6	$6765.9	$12230.3
ODA, net	611.1	1011.0	1126.2	1147.7	1104.9	1424.4	2215.4	2637.5	3303.7	3169.8
Bilateral	477.8	765.2	880.4	850.4	753.0	899.3	1531.0	1921.2	1960.8	2260.4
Grants	170.6	220.1	198.6	201.7	184.9	236.7	383.4	560.2	652.6	810.4
Loans	307.2	545.1	681.8	648.7	568.1	662.6	1147.6	1361.0	1308.2	1450.0
Multilateral	133.3	245.8	245.8	297.3	352.0	525.2	684.4	716.3	1342.9	909.4
Other official flows, net	856.4	1178.9	788.9	1369.4	1333.4	1622.6	2152.6	210.1	1478.0	3022.6
Private, at market terms	1252.3	3647.5	1038.5	352.4	1548.1	2487.9	6335.5	4689.0	1957.8	6010.6
Total/GNP *(Percent)*	0.95	1.44	0.65	0.59	0.72	0.80	1.09	0.75	0.65	1.08
DAC average *(Percent)*	0.82	0.79	0.81	1.05	0.97	1.05	1.00	1.16	1.05	1.13
ODA/GNP *(Percent)*	0.21	0.25	0.25	0.23	0.20	0.21	0.23	0.26	0.32	0.28
DAC average *(Percent)*	0.24	0.30	0.33	0.35	0.33	0.31	0.32	0.34	0.37	0.35

Sources: 1963-67: OECD, DAC, *Development Assistance Efforts and Policies* (Paris), annual reviews; 1968-71: OECD, DAC, *Development Assistance* (Paris), annual reviews; 1972-81: OECD, DAC, *Development Cooperation* (Paris), annual reviews.

a Overseas Development Assistance.

b The "Other official flows" category was first introduced in 1968; figures for 1962-67 are estimated by DAC.

c Development Assistance Committee (OECD).

they were pursued by the Japanese government offered considerable scope for bargaining to the potential beneficiaries, who were able to extract commitments for the development of regional infrastructure as part of the package. It was the financial requirements for the development of infrastructure which necessitated a larger percentage of aid in the form of grants. More recently emphasis has been placed on meeting basic human needs but (as discussed in further detail below) this new policy direction has yet to be reflected in a significant change in the overall sectoral allocation of aid funds.

(4) *Geographical*: A redirection of aid toward countries which were regarded as potentially important sources of raw materials. As will be discussed in more detail below, this led to an increasing share of aid being directed toward Latin America, the Middle East, and Africa.

In May 1978 Prime Minister Takeo Fukuda announced that his government would double overseas development assistance in the next three years—implicitly acknowledging the inadequacy of Japan's aid. This target was easily achieved: development assistance increased by 55 percent in 1978, 19 percent in 1979, and 16 percent in 1980. Some of this increase was artificial—for example, aid is reported in U.S. dollars; a rising exchange rate for the yen was reflected in larger dollar figures for the same volume of committed resources. However, the ODA/GNP ratio increased from 0.23 percent in 1978 to 0.32 percent in 1980. In 1979 the ratio exceeded that of the United States for the first time; Japan was now the fourth most important donor among OECD countries.

Although by the end of the 1980 fiscal year Japanese aid was more than double the total in 1977, Japan's ODA/GNP ratio remained below the OECD's DAC average. In response to continued overseas criticism, the government announced in 1980 that in the next five-year period it would double the total assistance it had given in 1976-80. This commitment is less generous than it appears: the low level of aid in 1976 and 1977 drags down the average target for 1981-86. Even if the new policy is fully implemented, aid will grow at a much slower rate than in the past: an average of 8.7 percent each year, compared to an annual increase of 32 percent over the 1977-80 period.

Early indications of the government's ability to implement the new policy are not encouraging. In 1981 Japanese ODA fell both in absolute terms and as a percentage of GNP. Although government expenditure in 1981 increased by over 5.8 percent, ODA fell by $225 million (6.7 percent). Only in the cases of Australia and the United States among OECD countries did overseas aid fall by more than this in 1981. The ODA/GNP ratio fell back to 0.28 percent. Japan slipped back among OECD countries both in terms of its ODA/GNP ratio and the grant element in its assistance. In part this decline was the result of the falling exchange rate for the yen, and in part, delays in Japan's payments to multilateral agencies. Aid was one of only four categories of expenditure scheduled to increase in 1982; however, even if the government implemented its promise to increase aid by 11 percent in 1982, the program for doubling expenditure by 1985 would remain behind schedule.

Despite recent efforts toward liberalization of the terms on which aid is given, Japan lags behind the DAC average on a number of dimensions: the average maturity of the loans, the average interest rate charged on loans, and the grant element as share of total ODA (see Table 4-2). Although loans from the Japanese government are

Table 4-2

EVOLUTION OF FINANCIAL TERMS OF ODA COMMITMENTS: JAPAN, UNITED STATES, AND DAC AVERAGE, 1970-79

Financial Term	Japan			United States			DAC Average		
	1970	1975	1979	1970	1975	1979	1970	1975	1979
Length of loans (*Years*)	21.4	26.7	27.7	37.4	37.0	37.0	29.9	32.6	31.2
Average rate of interest (*Nominal percent*)	3.7	3.1	3.1	2.6	2.6	2.8	2.8	2.5	2.6
Grant element as share of total ODA commitments (*Percent*)	67	69	78	87	86	75	84	89	77

Sources: 1968-71: OECD, DAC, *Development Assistance*, pp. 62-63; 1975: OECD, DAC, *Development Cooperation*, 1976, pp. 83, 158; 1979: OECD, DAC, *Development Cooperation*, 1980, Table B-1.

granted for much shorter periods than those granted by the United States, the terms of Japanese aid are becoming more similar to those for U.S. aid, in part because the United States in recent years has moved away from the DAC average toward the less liberal policies of Japan.

Table 4-3 contrasts the tying status of Japanese aid with that of the United States and with average DAC figures. By 1981 Japan's record—with the exception of grants—had not only surpassed that of the United States, but also was superior to the average performance of DAC member countries. It remains the case (as, to some extent, it does in the United States) that the role played by the private sector in the nomination of projects ensures that a large percentage of the contracts arising from Japanese aid will be won by domestic companies. For example, an official of Mitsubishi in the Tokyo interviews noted that his company had played a prominent role in arranging Japanese finance for new airports in Kenya and Malawi and had subsequently benefited from construction contracts for the projects. However, foreign aid proposals from recipient countries are increasingly being considered, despite Japanese frustration with the time it takes LDCs to come up with viable proposals.

In terms of Japanese self-interest in aid-giving, telling comparisons are derived from an examination of the sectoral allocation of bilateral ODA commitments (see Table 4-4). A larger percentage of Japanese ODA is devoted to the sector of industry, mining, and construction than is that of any other DAC country. Only West Germany approaches Japan's figure, which was more than double the DAC average. Japan accounted for 35 percent of total aid from OECD countries to this sector in 1981. Japan also gave the largest share among DAC donors to public utility development (infrastructure)—45 percent of its aid went to this sector, compared with a DAC average of 28.2 percent. A marked contrast is found in the Japanese contribution to health, education, and welfare in developing countries. Although (as noted) a larger proportion of Japanese aid has been devoted to "basic human needs" in recent years, the Japanese contribution to these sectors remains the least generous of any DAC donor. In 1981 less than 12 percent of total Japanese aid was given to these sectors; the average for all DAC countries was over 28 percent, and the U.S. figure more than 34 percent. In 1981 the United States accounted for close to a third of all aid given by DAC countries for health projects.

Table 4-3

TYING STATUS OF ODA: JAPAN, UNITED STATES, AND DAC AVERAGE, 1981

(Percent of gross disbursements)

ODA Donor	Bilateral ODA						Multilateral ODA		Total (Average)		
	Grants			Loans							
	Untied	Part Tied	Tied	Untied	Part Tied	Tied	Untied	Tied	Untied	Part Tied	Tied
Japan	33.3%	7.6%	59.1%	38.4%	27.7%	33.9%	100.0%	0.0%	53.2%	15.9%	30.9%
United States	28.3	17.0	54.7	14.4	13.2	72.4	90.7	9.3	38.8	12.1	49.1
DAC Average[a]	44.8	6.5	48.7	35.6	15.9	48.5	95.1	4.9	50.3	7.1	37.1

Source: Calculated from data in OECD, DAC, *Development Cooperation*, 1982, p. 191.

[a]DAC averages exclude EC multilateral aid (EDF), which is tied to procurement in the EC or ACP states (5.5 percent of DAC total).

Table 4-4

BREAKDOWN OF BILATERAL ODA COMMITMENTS BY SECTOR:
JAPAN, UNITED STATES, AND DAC AVERAGE, 1975 AND 1981
(*Percent*)

Sector	1975			1981		
	Japan	United States	DAC Average	Japan	United States	DAC Average
Planning and public administration	0.5%	1.5%	1.7%	0.5%	0.9%	1.9%
Public utility development	54.5	8.9	20.8	45.0	13.5	28.2
Agriculture	9.0	32.5	14.4	16.8	28.7	17.0
Industry, mining, construction	23.3	8.5	10.5	19.0	2.7	8.7
Trade, banking, tourism, etc.	2.6	2.2	2.6	0.8	0.1	1.0
Education	2.1	7.3	18.7	3.5	10.5	16.1
Health	1.0	14.7	7.7	7.4	16.2	8.3
Social infrastructure, welfare	0.2	9.3	6.6	0.4	7.7	4.3
Multi-sector	3.3	9.9	3.6	2.2	0.1	3.9
Unspecified	3.4	5.3	13.4	4.3	19.8	10.6

Sources: OECD, DAC, *Development Cooperation*, 1976, pp. 236-37, and 1982, pp. 230-31.

In contrast to its record on ODA, Japan's record of total flow of resources to developing countries and multilateral agencies has been above the DAC average in most years since 1969. Two factors contribute to this. The first is a consistent Japanese commitment to the support of multilateral agencies. Rix points to the importance that Japan accorded the United Nations as the basis of its postwar foreign policy. Despite concern expressed by the Ministry of Foreign Affairs that in multilateral aid donors were not identified and there-fore Japan would not be credited, such aid was popular as a means of divorcing aid from Cold War political considerations. Japan has con-tributed to over thirty UN-sponsored programs and to six multilateral financial institutions: the World Bank and its subsidiaries (the International Development Association and the International Finance Corporation) and three regional development banks (the Asian Development Bank, the Inter-American Development Bank, and the African Development Fund).[5]

The second and more important factor has been the prominent position of "Other official flows"—a DAC category denoting flows which are designed primarily to promote the donor's exports or overseas investments. The single most important item in this classification is official export credits. A quite startling statistic (which could be calculated from Table 4-1) is that export credits provided by the Japanese government have exceeded the value of its aggregate ODA in all but three years. Japan has at times been the principal OECD supplier of official export credits. In 1981, for instance, Japan provided 62 percent of all export credits originating in DAC countries; in the same year it was the origin of 12.4 percent of all ODA from DAC countries, and 12.3 percent of all private flows. Table 4-5 contrasts the share of other official flows in total Japanese official transfers compared with equivalent figures for the United States and all DAC member countries.

Table 4-5

RATIO OF OTHER OFFICIAL FLOWS TO TOTAL OFFICIAL TRANSFERS:
JAPAN, UNITED STATES, AND DAC AVERAGE, 1971-81
(*Percent*)

Trade Partner	1971-73 Average	1978	1979	1980	1981
Japan	62.3%	60.5%	49.1%	47.8%	57.8%
United States	20.9	27.1	34.5	28.8	31.9
DAC Average	27.7	30.1	27.9	29.0	30.6

Source: OECD, DAC, *Development Cooperation*, 1982, p. 219.

JAPANESE AID TO AFRICA

Early Japanese ODA was focused almost exclusively on Asia, the area with which it had the most familiarity and which contained its principal Third World trading partners. The first loans to African countries were not made until 1966—several years after many had received their independence. Uganda was the first African country to receive a Japanese loan, followed in the same year by Kenya, Nigeria, and Tanzania. As Table 4-6 shows, Africa as a whole was receiving only 1 percent of Japanese ODA by the end of the 1960s. Rix provides a succinct summary of Japanese attitudes toward Africa before the 1970s:

Africa was regarded by aid officials in Japan as distant and difficult to deal with. They complained, rightly or wrongly, that Africans thought differently from Southeast Asians and that aid negotiations were correspondingly more protracted. They predicted that these difficulties would not soon diminish, despite growing aid flows to the region. Japanese knew little about Africa and about the conditions upon which aid requests were made, and loan officials cited this as one reason why decisions on aid to Africa might take much longer than on similar requests from Asian countries. At a more materialistic level, they perceived that trading benefits to Japan from aid to Africa were insufficient to warrant a shift in priorities. Africa was regarded as something like the "dark continent" into which Japanese aid disappeared with no acknowledgement of its origins. . . . In short, prevailing attitudes towards countries in Africa as recipients only strengthened the bias in favor of Asia and the established decision-making and information-gathering procedures.[6]

Japan's lack of familiarity with Africa did not prevent the continent from becoming a major recipient of both private and public overseas flows from Japan (Table 4-7). A principal reason for this was Africa's share in official and private export credits from Japan, as seen in Table 4-8. At times in the mid-1960s Africa accounted for over one third of these flows—primarily a reflection of export credits extended to Japanese shipping companies operating in Liberia. In the 1970s a smaller proportion of these credits was directed to Africa—a

JAPANESE OVERSEAS DEVELOPMENT ASSISTANCE

Table 4-6

GEOGRAPHICAL DISTRIBUTION OF JAPAN'S BILATERAL ODA,[a] 1963-81

Year[b]	Total Flows (Millions of dollars)	Regional Distribution (Percent)			
		Asia	Middle East and North Africa	Central and South America	Sub-Saharan Africa
1963	$ 128	98.7%	0.3%	0.4%	0.3%
1965	226	98.1	0.2	0.6	0.6
1967	346	97.6	0.2	0.7	0.8
1969	340	100.0	0.8	-3.9	1.2
1971	432	98.4	0.9	-2.6	3.0
1973	765	88.1	0.3	4.6	2.4
1975	850	75.1	10.0	5.6	6.9
1977	899	59.3	24.5	8.8	6.3
1978	1,531	60.3	22.7	8.6	6.9
1979	1,921	69.3	10.6	8.6	9.7
1980	1,961	70.5	10.4	6.0	11.4[c]
1981	2,260	71.0	8.4	7.8	9.3[c]

Sources: 1963-67: Rix, *Japan's Economic Aid*, p. 34; QECD, DAC, *Development Assistance Efforts and Policies*; 1968-71: OECD, DAC, *Development Assistance*; 1969-81: MITI, "Economic Cooperation of Japan," 1980, 1981, 1982 (mimeo); 1972-81: OECD, DAC, *Development Cooperation*.

[a] Grants or loans at below market rates.

[b] We list only the years reported in Rix for the period before 1977.

[c] Excludes Sudan.

Table 4-7

GEOGRAPHICAL DISTRIBUTION OF JAPAN'S BILATERAL ECONOMIC
COOPERATION: ODA, OTHER OFFICIAL FLOWS,[a]
AND PRIVATE TRANSFERS, 1963-81

		Regional Distribution (Percent)			
Year[b]	Total Flows (Millions of dollars)	Asia	Middle East and North Africa	Central and South America	Sub-Saharan Africa
1963	$ 369	56.0%	8.0%	10.3%	16.4%
1965	705	53.4	1.9	13.4	22.4
1967	894	58.6	8.1	5.2	23.3
1969	1,128	73.8	9.5	6.7	4.9
1971	1,688	64.1	5.6	16.6	8.6
1973	5,032	39.1	2.7	46.1	7.6
1975	2,560	60.3	12.9	18.4	6.8
1977	4,536	28.0	13.8	25.2	22.9
1978	8,949	31.3	14.2	30.2	20.4
1979	6,330	43.3	2.9	27.4	18.7
1980	5,191	N.A.	N.A.	N.A.	9.4[c]
1981	9,571	N.A.	N.A.	N.A.	8.5[c]

Sources: Same as Table 4-6.

[a]Includes export credits.

[b]We list only the years reported in Rix for the period before 1977.

[c]Excludes Sudan.

Table 4-8

GEOGRAPHICAL DISTRIBUTION OF JAPAN'S BILATERAL ECONOMIC
COOPERATION: OTHER OFFICIAL FLOWS[a] AND PRIVATE
TRANSFERS ONLY, 1963-81

Year[b]	Total Flows (Millions of dollars)	Regional Distribution (Percent)			
		Asia	Middle East and North Africa	Central and South America	Sub-Saharan Africa
1963	$ 241	33.5%	14.1%	13.5%	29.1%
1965	479	32.3	3.2	17.0	37.6
1967	548	33.8	14.8	9.7	42.7
1969	788	62.5	13.1	11.2	6.4
1971	1,256	52.3	7.3	23.2	10.5
1973	4,267	30.4	3.2	53.4	8.5
1975	1,710	53.0	14.0	24.8	6.7
1977	3,637	17.8	14.6	30.0	25.0
1978	7,418	25.3	25.8	34.7	9.8
1979	4,409	32.0	13.6	35.6	8.6
1980	3,230	N.A.	N.A.	N.A.	8.2[c]
1981	7,311	N.A.	N.A.	N.A.	8.3[c]

Sources: Same as Table 4-6.

[a]Includes export credits.

[b]We list only the years reported in Rix for the period before 1977.

[c]Excludes Sudan.

reflection not only of the depression in world shipping following the OPEC oil embargo, but also of Japan's interest in resource projects in Latin America, North Africa, and the Middle East. Nonetheless, at the end of March 1980 sub-Saharan Africa still accounted for 21 percent of the cumulative postwar total of $75 billion worth of Japanese deferred payment exports. Eighty-six percent of this was the result of shipping exports; of the remaining items only industrial machinery (10.5 percent) made a significant contribution to the aggregate figure.[7]

The first OPEC shock to the world economy in 1973 moved Japan to increase its foreign aid to Africa. The shock reinforced Japanese perceptions of vulnerabilities to curtailments of raw materials supplies and led to a frantic scramble to diversify sources. It led to a new awareness of and interest in the African continent, underlined in 1974, when Toshio Kimura became the first Japanese Foreign Minister to visit Africa while in office. Africa, with its preponderance of LDCs, has also been favored in recent years in Japanese aid as Tokyo has sought to answer criticism from the Third World that insufficient attention was being given in its aid program to countries most in need. Consequently Japanese aid to Africa has increased substantially over the last decade, both as regards Africa's share in Japanese ODA (which rose to over 10 percent), and in absolute terms, with aid amounting to $210 million in 1981. By the beginning of the 1980s Africa's share in Japanese aid was roughly equivalent to its share in total U.S. economic assistance. (See Table E-1 in Appendix E. For purposes of comparison Appendix E includes a table detailing total U.S. official assistance to Black Africa in the period 1946-82.)

Despite recent diversification, Japanese aid is heavily concentrated on a limited number of favored recipients. Aid receipts are highly correlated with the importance of the country in Japan's trade with the continent and with the recipient's potential for supplying raw materials to Japan. There is therefore a close relationship between private and public flows from Japan to Africa (see Table 4-9). Although virtually all African countries have received some Japanese aid, eight—Kenya, Madagascar, Niger, Nigeria, Sudan, Tanzania, Zaire, and Zambia—shared more than 70 percent of all Japanese aid to sub-Saharan Africa in the period 1960-81. Zaire, Zambia, and Niger are major suppliers of critical raw materials to the Japanese economy (primarily copper and uranium). In Madagascar, Japan has significant investments in the mining of chromium ore and in the fishing industry. Similarly, Sudan is a potential source of chromium; Mitsubishi and the Japan Metals and Chemicals Company have invested $50-60 million in exploration and mining activities in the Ingessana Hills. Some of the Japanese aid has been designed to facilitate the exploitation of mineral deposits—e.g., the Japanese-financed railroad from Lumumbashi to Matadi.

Two recipients which are not major sources of raw materials for the Japanese economy are Kenya and Tanzania. According to Japanese aid officials in the Tokyo interviews, Japan places emphasis on these countries in its aid-giving because of their geopolitical importance and their prominent roles as representatives of African opinion. Furthermore, both countries are favored because of their relative proximity to Japan and because Japanese officials find it easier to deal with English-speaking Africa. Kenya is regarded favorably because of the relative openness of its economy toward the West; the officials also commented that Nairobi was a pleasant and convenient place to be based. Tanzania is one of Africa's poorest countries, and Japan can point to its aid activities there in answer to criticism that it does little for the world's least developed. In addition, Tokyo has become increasingly concerned at the Soviet presence in the Indian Ocean. Officials in the Japanese Ministry of Foreign Affairs perceive a division of labor emerging in which the United States may concentrate its efforts on Kenya and Somalia, while Japan may focus on Tanzania. (Aid officials suggested that strategic considerations would be increasingly important in the distribution of Japanese aid in the 1980s.) Both Kenya and Tanzania are also important trading partners for Japan on the African continent, and with both Japan enjoys a favorable balance of trade of significant proportions. (For example, in 1981 Japanese exports to Kenya exceeded imports by a ratio of more than 10 to 1.)

Francophone Africa has been underrepresented in Japan's aid to the continent, a result both of language difficulties and Japanese perceptions of a relatively closed Francophone·community. Language has not been a barrier, however, in countries where Japan has mineral interests—notably Niger and Zaire—although aid officials noted in the Tokyo interviews that significant difficulties had been experienced in implementing projects in Zaire. It was suggested that Japan is unlikely to undertake any major projects there once current commitments are completed.

Table 4-9

CUMULATIVE JAPANESE OFFICIAL AND PRIVATE TRANSFERS TO
AFRICAN COUNTRIES, 1960-81
(Millions of dollars)

Country	Official Transfers	Private Transfers	Total
Angola	$ 0.05	$ 1.84	$ 1.89
Benin	2.27	0.00	2.27
Botswana	1.83	0.00	1.83
Burundi	4.96	0.00	4.96
Cameroon	0.56	−0.06	0.50
Cape Verde	2.89	0.00	2.89
Central African Republic	3.44	0.00	3.44
Chad	0.02	0.00	0.02
Comoros	1.99	−0.36	1.63
Congo	0.82	1.27	2.09
Djibouti	0.02	0.00	0.02
Equatorial Guinea	N.A.	N.A.	N.A.
Ethiopia	24.20	6.15	30.35
Gabon	10.96	82.30	93.26
Gambia	1.01	0.19	1.20
Ghana	30.04	19.89	49.93
Guinea	11.55	21.32	32.87
Guinea Bissau	1.42	−1.33	0.09
Ivory Coast	4.21	67.38	71.59
Kenya	132.64	37.20	169.84
Lesotho	0.69	0.00	0.69
Liberia	25.97	2592.77	2618.74
Madagascar	65.94	8.94	74.88

Table 4-9 (cont.)

Country	Official Transfers	Private Transfers	Total
Malawi	$ 34.11	$ 11.90	$ 46.01
Mali	17.42	0.00	17.42
Mauritania	7.14	3.72	10.86
Mozambique	7.69	20.02	27.71
Niger	46.50	95.09	141.59
Nigeria	76.26	84.34	160.60
Rwanda	20.71	0.58	21.29
Sao Tome and Principe	0.11	0.00	0.11
Senegal	21.15	11.70	32.85
Seychelles	0.13	0.06	0.19
Sierra Leone	21.32	-1.66	19.66
Somalia	2.83	0.00	2.83
Sudan	66.37	N.A.	N.A.
Swaziland	2.19	2.20	4.39
Tanzania	130.81	47.21	178.02
Togo	3.01	0.00	3.01
Uganda	8.27	0.76	9.03
Upper Volta	2.88	1.15	4.03
Zaire	126.32	275.60	401.92
Zambia	101.49	150.57	252.06
Zimbabwe	3.44	0.56	4.00
Others	5.50	11.79	17.29
TOTAL	1041.70	3550.62	4592.32

Sources: Same as Table 4-1.

Despite recent increases, Japanese aid to Africa plays a relatively minor role in total African receipts of ODA from DAC countries. Europe continues to be the principal source of aid for sub-Saharan Africa. In 1979 the Japanese share in total receipts was merely 6.5 percent. Only in seven cases—Guinea, Kenya, Madagascar, Niger, Nigeria, Sudan, and Zambia—did the Japanese contribution amount to more than 10 percent of an African country's total aid receipts from OECD states (see Table 4-10). In comparison, the U.S. share in total African receipts was 14 percent. It is noteworthy, however, that Japanese aid exceeded that from the United States in ten African states (including such important countries as Kenya, Nigeria, and Tanzania).

Table 4-10

COMPARISON OF JAPANESE AND U.S. SHARES IN OECD ODA
TO AFRICA, 1979
(*Percent*)

Country	Share of ODA		Country	Share of ODA	
	Japan	United States		Japan	United States
Angola	0.0%	6.8%	Mali	0.0%	14.9%
Benin	0.0	6.2	Mauritania	0.6	16.9
Botswana	0.3	8.2	Mozambique	3.2	16.5
Burundi	0.0	4.5	Niger	14.1	9.4
Cameroon	0.1	6.0	Nigeria	14.1	0.0
Central African			Rwanda	5.9	5.6
Republic	4.1	2.0	Senegal	2.3	18.1
Chad	0.0	22.2	Sierra Leone	0.7	21.3
Congo	0.0	0.0	Somalia	0.4	40.2
Gabon	0.4	0.0	Sudan	14.4	14.9
Gambia	3.2	15.2	Swaziland	0.9	6.3
Ghana	6.3	24.8	Tanzania	5.2	2.2
Guinea	20.4	35.2	Togo	0.3	7.3
Ivory Coast	0.1	1.4	Uganda	1.9	0.0
Kenya	12.3	5.6	Upper Volta	0.1	17.4
Lesotho	1.7	20.6	Zaire	9.5	15.2
Liberia	5.6	32.9	Zambia	11.1	20.3
Madagascar	27.9	4.1	Zimbabwe	0.0	0.0
Malawi	7.5	3.3			

Source: OECD, DAC, *Geographic Distribution of ODA Flows*, 1980.

It seems unlikely that Japan will play a more important role in African aid in the future. In recent years its geographical distribution of aid has stabilized, with 60 percent directed toward Asia, and 10 percent each toward the other major recipients: Latin America, the Middle East, and Africa. According to the Director-General of the Economic Cooperation Bureau in Japan's Foreign Ministry, the "pattern of ODA allocation is thought to be an appropriate one and is expected to prevail in future ODA allocations."[8]

Japan continues to find it difficult to implement its aid policies in Africa. Officials in the Tokyo interviews noted Japan's lack of familiarity with African culture, which contrasted with its relative ease of dealing with Asian countries. They also expressed concern at the lack of viable projects in many African countries. The disbursement ratio in Africa was low owing to the difficulties of implementing projects. Moreover, there was a perception among some officials that the effectiveness of Japanese aid in Africa was low, in part because it was spread too thinly over a large number of countries. (Japan has aid missions in only fourteen countries, and these are responsible for the entire continent.) Accordingly, it was asserted, despite continued pressure for further diversification of Japanese aid, it is likely that in the 1980s Japan will maintain its concentration on countries identified as important to its interests—namely, Kenya, Niger, Nigeria, Tanzania, Zaire, Zambia, and Zimbabwe.

Chapter 5

JAPANESE AND U.S. GOVERNMENT PROGRAMS IN SUPPORT OF OVERSEAS COMMERCIAL ACTIVITIES

Our analysis of trade relations in Chapter 2 suggested that Japanese exporters over the last decade have been much more successful than their U.S. competitors in penetrating the African market. This type of analysis is unable to isolate the causes of relative success and failure. Indeed even the most sophisticated econometric model can only hint at the reasons which underlie different performances in export markets. Many factors may be involved—the quality and pricing of a particular product, relative exchange rates, the availability of information on business opportunities, the willingness of entrepreneurs to take risks in new markets and/or to bribe local officials, and the government policies which serve to promote or deter foreign trade and investment.

Domestic economic policies may have important repercussions for the foreign activities of local corporations. For instance, in the area of foreign investment, Japanese firms operating overseas are said to be at an advantage vis-à-vis their American counterparts because of a lower interest rate structure in Japan which reduces their interest burden in international transactions (see below). It is often claimed that the yen is undervalued—a charge that, if accurate, would have both positive and negative implications for Japan's overseas commercial activities. While undervaluation would stimulate Japanese exports by making them cheap relative to those of their major competitors, it would act as a deterrent to Japanese overseas investment by making it more expensive to purchase foreign assets.

This chapter explores the various programs that are offered by the governments of Japan and the United States in support of the overseas commercial activities of their respective private sectors. While governments can themselves directly do little about the quality of products offered by exporters, they can intervene to make export prices more competitive and to reduce the risks borne by overseas traders and investors. Whether they do so successfully can have a significant impact on the success of their private sectors.

Table 5-1 presents a comparison of Japanese and U.S. government programs in support of overseas investment and trade. Japan's extensive range of government instruments for export promotion is coordinated by two agencies, the Japanese EXIM Bank and MITI (primarily through its export insurance division). In addition, a number of smaller programs are administered by various specialized agencies, including the Metal Mining Agency, the Japan Petroleum Development Corporation, the Overseas Uranium Resources Development Company, and the Overseas Economic Cooperation Fund.

SUPPORT PROGRAMS OF THE JAPANESE AND U.S. EXIM BANKS

The EXIM Bank of Japan (referred to as EXIM), an independent government agency established in 1950, provides buyer and supplier credits to supplement commercial bank financing of Japanese exports. No credits are available for terms of less than one year (but short-term loans may be rediscounted by the Bank of Japan at its official discount rate plus a premium of 0.25 percent). Fixed-rate financing is available for medium- and long-term transactions. The EXIM Bank normally limits its participation to 50-60 percent of the financed amount, with the balance provided by Japanese commercial banks, which are repaid *pari passu* with the EXIM Bank.

Loans were traditionally extended only to suppliers, but in recent years buyer credits and bank-to-bank loans have also been made available. Funding is provided only in yen, but MITI's Export Insurance Division has since 1974 provided an exchange risk insurance program covering loans denominated in U.S. dollars, sterling, French francs, German marks, and Swiss francs. During the first two years of the repayment period (maximum fifteen years), the supplier bears all exchange risks and may cover these in the forward market. In the event of depreciation of the currency of repayment against the yen, the supplier must bear the first 3 percent of any exchange rate loss. MITI's maximum liability is 20 percent. Coverage is limited to specific product groups, which include plant and equipment, ships, aircraft, and engineering services. The MITI program appears to have been little

Table 5-1

COMPARISON OF JAPANESE AND U. S. GOVERNMENT SUPPORT
PROGRAMS FOR OVERSEAS ECONOMIC ACTIVITIES

| | Institutions | |
Program	Japan	United States
Export financing	EXIM Bank export credits	EXIM Bank Private Export Funding Corporations (PEFCO)
Export earnings insurance	MITI export earnings insurance	Foreign Credit Insurance Association (FCIA)
Overseas investment insurance	MITI overseas investment insurance	Overseas Private Investment Corporation (OPIC)
Overseas investment financing (loan funds, preferential loan terms, foreign currency loans)	EXIM Bank loans Metal Mining Agency Japan Petroleum Development Corporation Overseas Uranium Resources Development Company Japanese Overseas Trade Development Corporation Shoko Chukin Bank Overseas Economic Cooperation Fund	OPIC
Information dissemination	JETRO Japanese Embassy MITI	U.S. Embassy Foreign Commercial Service
Tax incentives for overseas investment and trade	Write-offs for overseas investment losses Tax reductions for overseas direct investment Importation of natural resources	Domestic International Sales Corporation (DISC)

used: exporters instead have preferred to cover risks through foreign exchange forward markets or have them underwritten by the trading companies.

In addition to this conventional export credit program, EXIM provides a number of other supports for Japanese traders. Most important of these are import credits, overseas investment credits, and overseas direct loans. Import credits are provided over the long term to Japanese importers of vital resources and other items regarded as important by the government. The primary objective has been to facilitate the development of natural resource deposits overseas which will eventually produce for the Japanese market. Eligible products include (a) energy resources, including petroleum, natural gas, coal, and uranium; (b) mineral resources such as iron ore, copper, and aluminum; (c) other raw materials, including lumber and salt; and (d) other strategic imports such as aircraft. Normally loans under the import credits program are of five- to seven-year duration and provide for up to 70 percent of the proposed capital spending of a project.

Overseas investment credits are provided by the EXIM Bank to Japanese investors in order to allow them to participate in (a) equity investment in foreign corporations; (b) long-term loans to foreign entities for projects overseas; (c) loans to foreign entities to finance their equity interest in foreign firms, which also have equity participation from Japanese investors; (d) equity investment in another Japanese entity whose sole function is to make overseas investments; and (e) funds required for projects overseas which are directly operated by the Japanese borrower. In a typical year over 80 percent of these credits are given to natural resource projects.

Overseas direct loans take three forms: (a) buyers' credits; (b) bank-to-bank loans; and (c) government-to-government loans. Buyers' credits and bank-to-bank loans have become increasingly important means of financing plant exports in recent years. In addition, substantial sums in untied loans have been provided for resource development projects and for assistance to international development banks (e.g., a $41 million loan to the African Development Bank in 1981). Direct government-to-government loans have been provided to assist economic development projects (e.g., loans in 1978 to Zambia and Nigeria for [respectively] the expansion of radio and TV networks and the provision of a transportable electric power-generating plant). However, no new government-to-government loans have been provided since 1978.

EXIM initially doubled as Japan's aid agency and still occasionally combines with the Overseas Economic Cooperation Fund to provide mixed credits—i.e., export credits and concessional loans. Mixed credits have been particularly important in the promotion of natural resource projects in developing countries. Japan has also been willing to provide local cost support to purchasers of Japanese exports, perceiving that this is an important component of projects in developing countries. In the case of both local cost support and mixed credits, Japan has complied with the guidelines established by the OECD for such programs.

Tables 5-2 through 5-6 provide data on the regional breakdown of support provided by Japan's EXIM from 1969 to 1981. As Table 5-2 shows, Africa's share in total credit commitments has fluctuated considerably over the period, although the overall trend has been downward. In part, this is explained by the decline in credits for ships "exported" to Liberia in the 1970s. (In reality, of course, such "exports" were primarily a means of supporting the domestic shipbuilding industry; the ships were "exported" merely in the sense of being registered in Liberia by Japanese shipping companies based there.)[1] Africa's share of export credits for industrial plant rose substantially in 1979—largely, one presumes, because of Nigerian purchases—but it has subsequently declined quite dramatically. Unfortunately data are not available for individual African countries; moreover, the African regional classification employed by Japan's EXIM includes north Africa (but not the Middle East, which is classified as part of "Asia").

In general, Africa has not had a major share of import credits granted by EXIM—a reflection of the relatively unimportant role of the continent in supplying raw materials to Japan. Nor has Africa figured prominently in overseas investment credits. In contrast, in 1978 and 1979 Africa was the most favored region for overseas direct loans; again, however, these have fallen off in recent years, primarily as a result of the curtailment of the government-to-government loans program.

Africa's 11 percent share in the Japanese EXIM's total loans outstanding of $22.5 billion in 1982 was similar to its 12 percent share in the total exposure of the U.S. EXIM Bank of $28.7 billion in 1979. Given the larger overall size of the U.S. program, more support for exports from the United States to the continent has been provided

Table 5-2

JAPANESE EXIM BANK: TOTAL CREDIT COMMITMENTS
BY AREA, 1969-81
(*Percent*)

Year	Africa[a]	Oceania	Europe	Central and South America	North America	Middle East and Asia
1969	30%	4%	23%	8%	2%	32%
1970	27	7	19	7	7	32
1971	23	4	20	10	3	30
1972	21	0	28	18	16	14
1973	16	4	12	27	18	23
1974	8	3	28	16	11	32
1975	10	1	19	15	4	48
1976	17	2	22	23	1	34
1977	18	3	26	10	4	39
1978	17	3	13	12	31	24
1979	18	7	22	20	9	24
1980	9	8	20	8	4	50
1981	6	6	23	17	3	44
Total loans outstanding as of 3/31/82 ($22.5 billion)	11	3	17	15	10	42

Source: Export-Import Bank of Japan, *Annual Reports*, 1970-82.

[a]Includes north Africa.

Table 5-3

JAPANESE EXIM BANK: EXPORT CREDIT COMMITMENTS
BY AREA, 1969-81
(*Percent*)

Year	Africa[a]	Oceania	Europe	Central and South America	North America	Middle East and Asia
1969	33%	1%	28%	7%	2%	29%
1970	35	1	25	8	2	27
1971	34	1	29	10	1	25
1972	36	1	31	12	0	20
1973[b]	31	0	32	15	2	20
1974[b]	3	0	19	15	1	62
1975[b]	10	0	10	20	0	60
1976[b]	10	1	17	34	1	37
1977[b]	10	1	15	12	0	61
1978[b]	13	1	21	15	0	49
1979[b]	25	7	12	13	0	42
1980[b]	16	0	18	10	3	53
1981[b]	7	5	19	21	4	44
Cumulative total as of 3/31/82 ($28.7 billion)	N.A.	N.A.	N.A.	N.A.	N.A.	N.A.

Source: Same as Table 5-2.

[a]Includes north Africa.

[b]Figures refer only to credit commitments for plants (i.e., ships excluded).

JAPANESE/U.S. GOVERNMENT SUPPORT OF OVERSEAS COMMERCE

Table 5-4

JAPANESE EXIM BANK: IMPORT CREDIT COMMITMENTS
BY AREA, 1969-81
(*Percent*)

Year	Africa[a]	Oceania	Europe	Central and South America	North America	Middle East and Asia
1969	47%	5%	—	44%	—	4%
1970	—	20	—	10	57%	13
1971[b]	7	24	—	30	14	25
1977	—	10	—	—	38	52
1978	14	5	5%	10	61	5
1979	9	5	38	29	17	2
1980	—	—	—	—	56	44
1981	—	—	—	—	2	98
Cumulative total as of 3/31/82 ($8.1 billion)	N.A.	N.A.	N.A.	N.A.	N.A.	N.A.

Source: Same as Table 5-2.

[a]Includes north Africa.

[b]No figures available for 1972-76.

EMERGING JAPANESE ECONOMIC INFLUENCE IN AFRICA

Table 5-5

JAPANESE EXIM BANK: OVERSEAS INVESTMENT CREDITS
BY AREA, 1969-81
(*Percent*)

Year	Africa[a]	Oceania	Europe	Central and South America	North America	Middle East and Asia
1969	6%	41%	0%	1%	10%	42%
1970	0	34	1	3	16	46
1971	0	8	1	3	11	75
1972	0	1	67	10	3	20
1973	4	14	12	20	22	29
1974	0	6	7	18	3	66
1975	5	1	8	31	6	49
1976	10	13	2	10	4	61
1977	3	14	5	16	6	57
1978	12	4	2	6	2	85
1979	7	17	4	18	16	40
1980	2	35	4	3	11	44
1981	4	20	3	12	8	53
Cumulative total as of 3/31/82 ($7.4 billion)	3.3	15.4	7.1	13.2	9.9	51.1

Source: Same as Table 5-2.

[a]Includes north Africa.

96

Table 5-6

JAPANESE EXIM BANK: OVERSEAS DIRECT LOAN COMMITMENTS
BY AREA, 1975-81[a]

(Percent)

Year	Africa[b]	Oceania	Europe	Central and South America	North America	Middle East and Asia
1975	2%	—	46%	4%	—	35%
1976	15	—	23	34	—	24
1977	29	—	55	10	—	7
1978	45	—	30	20	—	1
1979	51	—	13	18	—	18
1980	2	—	30	9	—	59
1981	2	—	46	18	—	33
Cumulative total as of 3/31/82 ($11.3 billion)	9.2	0.4	31.3	18.1	0	37.6

Source: Same as Table 5-2.

[a]Loans include buyers' credits, bank-to-bank loans, and government-to-government loans.

[b]Includes north Africa.

than by the Japanese EXIM for the exports of its manufacturers. Nevertheless, support from the U.S. EXIM is more limited in scope than that of its major competitors, including Japan. The U.S. EXIM itself noted the following in its most recent report to Congress:

> By a substantial margin, the United States does not offer as wide a range of export support programs as do its major competitors. Moreover, with the virtual elimination of mixed credits (except in Egypt) and local cost support in 1981, the United States offered essentially only credit support. Eximbank has, however, offered very long repayment terms in selected cases to counter the offers of mixed credits from competitor countries.[2]

By offering mixed credits and local cost support, Japan's EXIM places its exporters at an advantage, particularly in the markets of the poorer developing countries which might otherwise be unable to meet the costs of export credit provided at prevailing market rates. Such supports would appear to be of particular importance for Africa given the need for long-term fixed interest credits for the development of raw materials projects and the complementary requirements for infrastructural financing. Another program available to Japanese exporters but not to their U.S. competitors is exchange risk insurance.

Perhaps as important as the relative breadth of the programs of Japan's EXIM is the gap between the rates of interest on its loans and those of its U.S. competitor. This stems from differences in the domestic prime rates in the two countries: in recent years that in Japan has been substantially below that of the United States as a result of Japan's lower rate of inflation and higher domestic savings propensity. Japan's domestic rates of interest have been so low, in fact, that under the most recent revision of the OECD International Agreement on Officially Supported Export Credits of July 1982, Japan is obliged to charge a higher rate for export credits than for domestic loans—0.3% above the domestic prime. Nonetheless, it can still provide export credits at rates considerably below those of the United States. Furthermore, since the interest rates for export credits are above those prevailing in the local market, the program's cost to the government has been minimal.

In 1979, 1980, and 1981 the effective annual interest rate for long-term loans to upper-income countries from Japan's EXIM was

7.85, 7.65, and 7.94 percent respectively. For the United States the comparable figures were 8.3, 8.60, and 9.82 percent. Japan's rates were the lowest and those of the United States were the highest among the "Big Five" of the OECD (Japan, the United States, France, Germany, and the United Kingdom). For the three years noted, the U.S. EXIM estimated that the subsidy commitment by the Japanese government per billion dollars of long-term export credits amounted to $7.3 million, $67.7 million, and $3.2 million respectively. For the United States the equivalent figures were $52.4 million, $115.9 million, and $160.3 million. Bankers and exporters surveyed by the U.S. EXIM rated its interest costs on loans as uncompetitive and ranked U.S. programs at the bottom of the list in comparison with their principal competitors.[3]

As a result of problems in the domestic economy, the U.S. EXIM in recent years has found itself with uncompetitive interest rates and an export credit program which involves costly subsidies. This has led to a substantial reduction in the number of funding authorizations. High interest rates coupled with cutbacks in funding have caused it to fall behind its Japanese counterpart both in current authorizations and in total loans outstanding. In 1981 Japan's EXIM granted credit authorizations amounting to $7.3 billion dollars; the figure for the U.S. EXIM was $5.4 billion. Total loans outstanding for the Japanese EXIM in 1981 amounted to $25.1 billion, compared with $15.8 billion for the United States.

As an attempt to circumvent its lack of funds, the U.S. EXIM has relied increasingly on the Private Export Funding Corporation (PEFCO). This is a private company owned by U.S. commercial banks and major industrial corporations; it was established in 1970 on the initiative of the Bankers' Association for Foreign Trade. PEFCO raises its own funds in the private capital markets for lending for medium and long terms to overseas purchasers of U.S. capital goods (normally providing 10-45 percent of the funding, with the balance provided by commercial banks). All PEFCO loans are covered by an unconditional EXIM guarantee on both principal and interest; EXIM participates in all PEFCO decisions. PEFCO's assistance to exporters is very limited, however. In 1981 it entered into only five new loan commitments, which totaled $120 million.

U.S. EXIM appears to have been slow in entering the Nigerian market, Black Africa's largest economy. In 1981 its exposure there was only $143 million—less than the loans outstanding to the Ivory Coast ($208 million) and under one quarter of total exposure in Zaire. More than twice the total loans to Nigeria had been advanced to a disastrous power line scheme at Inga-Shaba in Zaire ($380 million). The distribution of U.S. EXIM loans would appear to suggest poor commercial judgment on the part of the bank and/or the prominence of political criteria in the selection of projects to support on the African continent. EXIM's lack of involvement in the Nigerian market might be explained in part by its traditional caution on project selection: over the years it has preferred projects which are "self-liquidating"—i.e., those which will provide foreign exchange to facilitate the repayment of external loans. Consequently it has tended to shun import-substituting projects (which have been important in Nigeria's recent industrialization plans) or infrastructural schemes.[4]

Neither the Japanese nor the U.S. EXIM Bank currently lends to South Africa. The Tokyo government prohibited further Japanese loans in 1974; the Evans Amendment of 1978 to the charter of the U.S. EXIM stipulated that the bank cannot extend loans to the public sector in South Africa until the U.S. President determines that significant progress has been made in dismantling the apartheid system. For the private sector, loans are prohibited unless the Secretary of State certifies that the buyer is following enlightened practices regarding equal treatment of employees.

EXPORT INSURANCE

Export credit insurance to Japanese companies for short-term transactions is provided by the Export Insurance Division of MITI. Coverage is made available through two policy options: a comprehensive or whole-turnover policy, whereby a supplier insures all sales to one buyer, or a specific policy designed to cover individual transactions. The first option is more popular and carries a lower insurance premium because it requires insurance of good- as well as bad-risk situations. Political risks are covered for up to 95 percent of the value of the financed portion, and commercial risks for up to 60 percent (80 percent in the case of certain whole-turnover policies).

Coverage is also provided for medium- and long-term transactions through the Export Insurance Division's Export Proceeds Insurance program, which provides coverage of up to 95 percent for political risks and 90 percent for commercial risks for exports of capital goods, ships, goods required for construction projects, and specified services. In addition, private banks are protected against default on the part of a transaction which they finance through the Export Bill Insurance program, which provides coverage of up to 80 percent of face value for commercial and political risks.

A similar range of services for short-term transactions is provided for U.S. exporters by the Foreign Credit Insurance Association (FCIA), created by EXIM in 1961. The FCIA is an association of over fifty major U.S. insurance companies; it was established in part because of a desire to avoid competition between EXIM and the private sector in providing short-term finance for exports. All major policy decisions of the FCIA are subject to EXIM approval. Coverage of risk is more comprehensive than Japan's short-term policies: 90 percent of commercial risks and 100 percent of political risks.

FCIA also provides medium-term insurance with the same risk coverage. This is supplemented by EXIM's Medium-Term Bank Guarantee Program, which differs from the FCIA program in that it is available only to commercial banks rather than to exporters and banks alike. In addition, EXIM offers "financial guarantees" to private credit institutions which participate in financing long-term export transactions. These provide 100 percent political and commercial coverage of the amount guaranteed.

Although insurance to U.S. exporters provides for a greater coverage of risk, it does so at the cost of higher premiums. In 1981 the fee for Japan's short-term export credit insurance averaged 0.125 percent; the equivalent figure for the United States was 1.23 percent. U.S. programs are much smaller than their Japanese equivalents. In 1981 the U.S. EXIM authorized 2,459 FCIA insurance transactions totaling $5.9 billion and provided 635 bank guarantees for medium- and long-term loans totaling $557 million. In contrast, more than 606,000 transactions were accepted for coverage under MITI programs in 1981, with a total value in excess of $60 billion. More than 55 percent of Japan's total exports were covered by MITI insurance in that year, whereas FCIA/EXIM programs supported only 8.1 percent of U.S. exports.[5]

INVESTMENT GUARANTEES

Japan's Overseas Investment Insurance scheme, administered by MITI, provides coverage for the three principal categories of political risks faced by overseas investors: expropriation, war, and convertibility—essentially exchange control actions taken after the conclusion of the guarantee contract which prevent or delay the repatriation of profits and/or capital. Instituted in 1970 following the merger of two ineffective programs, the scheme has proved popular with Japanese investors. Coverage is provided for direct investment in the form of equity, long-term loans to and a guarantee for a joint venture or a management-controlled enterprise, and investments made by Japanese firms abroad for the acquisition of real estate, equipment, and the like. Moreover, coverage can be extended to portfolio investment and to long-term loans to and guarantees for an enterprise not under Japanese control if it is engaged in the exploitation of mineral resources, timber, or other specified goods to be exported to Japan under long-term supply contracts. In these cases the insurance also covers a nonpolitical risk: the "credit" risk of the bankruptcy or default of the borrower.

Coverage under the scheme applies to 100 percent of the principal and to profits (to a limit of 10 percent of the residual amount of investment). Normally the maximum length of coverage is fifteen years. For the three types of political risk the annual premium is 0.55 percent; if the policy also covers "credit" risks, the premium is 1.3 percent.

Similar insurance is provided for U.S. investors by the Overseas Private Investment Corporation (OPIC). Policies are issued for a maximum of twenty years and typically cover up to 270 percent of the value of the initial investment: 90 percent representing the investment itself and 180 percent covering earnings and interest accrued. However, fees are higher than those of the Japanese scheme: normally 0.3 percent for convertibility risks and 0.6 percent for expropriation and war coverage.

As with the other programs discussed, there are marked contrasts in the scale of the U.S. and Japanese schemes. At the end of 1980, OPIC was insuring investments amounting to $4.1 billion (or 7 percent of the total stock of U.S. investment in developing countries), while Japan's Overseas Investment Insurance scheme was covering total investments of $5.8 billion (or 53 percent of total Japanese investment in developing countries). OPIC activities have been limited by two restrictions imposed by the U.S. Congress. First, it can provide insurance only where a host country has signed investment guarantee agreements with the United States. In Africa this has prevented OPIC from operating in Angola, Djibouti, Equatorial Guinea, Guinea Bissau, Mozambique, and Zimbabwe. Second, Congress restricts OPIC operations to countries where per capita income is below a specified level—$2950 in 1981 (raised from $1000; in 1979 dollars). At present the only African country affected by this restriction is Gabon.

OVERSEAS INVESTMENT FUNDS

JAPAN

In addition to the Overseas Investment Credit and Overseas Direct Loan programs run by EXIM, a number of Japanese government agencies provide funds for private companies wishing to invest abroad:

MITI Programs. MITI oversees programs operated by several public corporations which are aimed at promoting overseas raw material supplies. These include precious metals (through the Metal Mining Agency); uranium (through the Overseas Uranium Resources Development Company); and petroleum (through the Japan Petroleum Development Corporation). Each of these agencies has funds which it makes available to corporations for the exploration and development of natural resource supplies. These resource-oriented agencies often work in conjunction with the EXIM Bank.

Japan Overseas Trade Development Corporation (JOTDC). This agency was established in 1972 to assist small- and medium-sized firms in overseas investment activities. It offers loans to cover the financial requirements of such enterprises taking part in joint venture projects initiated at the request of a government in a developing region. Loan terms are quite generous. No interest is charged, although a sum equivalent to 0.75 percent of the loan is levied annually as an expense fee. The loan period is generally up to twenty years (with repayments deferrable for up to seven years). Finance is provided for up to two thirds of the capital requirement (three fourths in some special cases) of joint projects.

Shoko Chukin Bank for Commerce and Industrial Cooperatives. This bank offers loans to help small and medium enterprises finance direct investments in overseas markets. In addition, jointly with government agencies, the bank accommodates other types of loans when necessary. These loans are normally repayable in five to seven years and are designated for cooperative members.

Foreign Currency Loan Programs. These programs are yet another unique feature of Japanese supports. Investment loan funds denominated in foreign currencies are provided by the government to firms wishing to make overseas investments. These funds, which include U.S. dollars, are provided through authorized foreign exchange banks and public corporations: the Japan Petroleum Development Corporation, the Metal Mining Agency, the Overseas Economic Cooperation Fund, and the EXIM Bank. Each of these institutions can lend individually or in conjunction with other authorized agencies. When foreign currency loans are made, the funds are obtained by selling yen on the Tokyo foreign exchange market. Under this system the foreign exchange risks often experienced by foreign investors are shifted to the government institution.

UNITED STATES

The only U.S. overseas investment fund program equivalent to the Japanese is OPIC's Direct Investment Fund (akin to JOTDC). It was established in 1969 with resources derived primarily from OPIC's subscribed capital (currently $50 million). The fund's objective is to facilitate private investment overseas when commercial financing is unavailable on appropriate terms. OPIC provides loans at fixed rates (close to those prevailing in long-term commercial money markets) and investment guarantees. It is common practice for a portion of the loans to be sold to private banks, enabling OPIC to circulate its limited funds more rapidly. Of the total finance portfolio held in 1982, 48 percent was for projects in Africa.

JAPANESE/U.S. GOVERNMENT SUPPORT OF OVERSEAS COMMERCE

TAXATION SYSTEM

JAPAN

The Japanese taxation system offers three principal types of incentives to foreign investors: (1) conditional tax write-offs; (2) reserves against overseas investment losses; and (3) deductions for taxes paid abroad.

If a Japanese firm experiences a capital loss on investments in the minerals and natural resources area, 50 percent of the loss can be written off against the current year's tax liability.

Under the system of reserves against overseas investment losses, domestic corporations making overseas investments in specified fields in developing countries are authorized to set aside a certain percentage of the invested amount as a reserve fund which is not subject to taxation. In principle reserves will be retained for the first five years; then they may be dissolved in equal annual installments over a five-year period and counted as profits.

The reserve program applies to several areas of overseas business activities. First, it can be used in agriculture, forestry, fisheries, marine culture, mining, construction, and manufacturing industries. Twelve percent of investments and loans may be set aside as reserves. Second, economic cooperation investments and loans are included in this scheme; 25 percent of these investments and loans may be set aside as reserves. Third, the reserve system applies to natural resource development projects, including petroleum and inflammable natural gas. In the case of minerals, coal, fluorite, marine plants and animals, lumber, feed grains, and oil-bearing fruit (soybeans, rapeseed, palm, and copra), 100 percent of the investments made during the prospecting stage and 40 percent of those made during the development stage can be set aside as reserves regardless of the region.

Foreign tax payments may be deducted from a firm's Japanese tax liability. Should a Japanese corporation be levied with a corporation tax on its income generated in a foreign country, a certain amount of Japanese corporate taxes will be deductible in specific cases in order to avoid double taxation. The foreign tax credit deduction system is applied to dividends received from overseas companies in which Japanese corporations have an equity interest of 25 percent or more.

UNITED STATES

American tax laws offer limited incentives for investment in developing countries since income earned in those countries is not treated more favorably than income earned elsewhere. However, the U.S. tax system provides two incentives for American corporations to invest abroad, especially in low tax rate countries.

First, the U.S. does not tax the income of a foreign subsidiary of a domestic corporation until the income is paid as a dividend to the parent company. This deferral has the effect of reducing the effective tax rate in foreign countries in which the total effective tax rate is less than the U.S. statutory rate.

Second, the United States employs the tax credit method, whereby a corporation includes dividends received from a foreign subsidiary in its taxable income and the tax is computed at the ordinary rates applicable to corporations. The tax is then reduced by the amount of tax levied in the country where the foreign subsidiary is located. Under this approach, foreign taxes are treated as if they were paid to the United States, which simply reduces the taxes by the amount to the foreign country where the income originated.[6]

The net effect of the U.S. tax system on investment abroad is somewhat ambiguous, however, because of counteracting provisions of the U.S. tax system:

1. Investment tax credits cannot be claimed on foreign investments.
2. Accelerated depreciation provisions generally do not apply to foreign investments.
3. Foreign losses are generally treated less favorably than domestic losses in the U.S. tax code since foreign subsidiaries cannot be included in a firm's consolidated tax return.[7]

INFORMATION COLLECTION AND DISSEMINATION

The principal Japanese government agencies involved in the collection and dissemination of information on international trading and investment opportunities are the Japan External Trade Organization (JETRO) and MITI. JETRO, a public corporation, was established in the 1950s to provide detailed information to Japanese manufacturers on export opportunities and changes in tariffs and product specifications and to assist in marketing new Japanese products. Although JETRO has public corporation status, it is in reality funded by MITI, from which it also draws most of its staff.[8] In sub-Saharan Africa, JETRO has nine offices—in Cameroon, Ethiopia, Ghana, Ivory Coast, Kenya, Nigeria, South Africa, Tanzania, and Zaire. JETRO's activities are supplemented by those of MITI itself, which (among other activities) conducts an annual survey of Japanese enterprises engaged in overseas investment and of the local host corporations. JETRO's work has been particularly important for smaller companies which lack their own commercial intelligence networks.

U.S. exporters receive help in this domain from U.S. embassies overseas and the recently formed Foreign Commercial Service. However, a recent survey of American businesses operating in Africa found that there was considerable dissatisfaction with the support provided by embassies for commercial activities. Often the support varied according to the personal interests of the ambassador; a number of companies preferred to have nothing to do with the local U.S. missions.[9] Nor was there much enthusiasm for the activities of the Foreign Commercial Service, which was perceived as being particularly neglectful of Africa. The service in principle has branches in Lagos, Kaduna, Kinshasa, Nairobi, Harare, Monrovia, and Accra, but the last two posts are vacant and unlikely to be filled.

UNITED STATES ANTI-TRUST LAW AND FOREIGN CORRUPT PRACTICES LEGISLATION

In recent years, Congressional concern over the business practices of American firms abroad has prompted legislative changes. Anti-trust legislation has been altered to promote U.S. commercial activities overseas while new laws have been enacted regarding the potential unfair business practices of U.S. firms operating abroad.

According to the Sherman Act, actions occurring in foreign countries which had substantial effects on domestic commerce were subject to U.S. anti-trust jurisdiction. In 1982, the Export Promotions Act (PL 97-290) clarified some uncertainty regarding the applicability of the Sherman Act with respect to trading companies formed for the sole purpose of engaging in export trade. Trading companies are exempted from the Sherman Act provisions as long as they do not "artificially enhance or depress prices" within the United States. The Export Promotions Act also permits bank holding companies to invest in such companies, and it further directs the Department of Commerce to create an office to promote the formation of export trade associations and companies.

The Foreign Corrupt Practices Act (PL 95-213) of 1977 resulted from growing public and Congressional concern over the use of bribery by U.S. multinational firms. The act prohibits the payment of money to officials of foreign governments to perform services of any kind. The penalties include fines up to $1 million and the treatment of bribes as income for tax purposes. Since the passage of the act there have been complaints within the American business community about the interpretation of certain of its provisions. Furthermore, uncertainty about the enforcement policies of the Department of Justice and the Securities and Exchange Commission have forced U.S. businesses to forego some overseas business opportunities.

CONCLUSIONS

In this chapter we have discussed ways in which governments can support the overseas activities of their private sectors. Government actions can serve equally to handicap such activities. U.S. corporations frequently complain that the government plays an adversarial rather than supportive role. In particular, they point to anti-trust legislation (which has prevented U.S. corporations from forming trading companies similar to their very successful Japanese competitors) and to the Foreign Corrupt Practices Act, which, it is alleged, makes business operations extremely difficult in a number of developing countries. Japanese corporations are not faced by similar legislation. In general, despite conflicts over specific policies, the working relationship between government and private sector in Japan is one of mutual support, the government placing no barriers in the way of overseas commercial activities. Tokyo's active support for Japanese trade and investment overseas may be contrasted with the official stance of the U.S. Department of Commerce, which maintains that the U.S. government neither encourages nor discourages foreign investment.

Chapter 6

SUMMARY AND CONCLUSIONS

Our detailed analysis of Japanese and U.S. economic relations with Africa has confirmed our initial impression that while the United States has become a relatively less important economic actor for the continent in recent years, Japan has considerably strengthened and diversified its economic ties. Japan's recent success in penetrating African markets was shown in our market share analysis in Chapter 2. Japan has matched the EC in its performance in retaining its share of African markets despite the fact that oil-importing African countries were, by the end of the period under consideration, of necessity spending a larger proportion of their foreign exchange on importing oil than was the case in the early years of the decade. Only in the markets of the two principal copper exporters (Zaire and Zambia), whose purchasing power was significantly eroded with the precipitous decline in copper prices, did Japan experience a decline in its market shares. In the case of Africa's oil exporters, Japan was successful in increasing its market share. It also increased its market share in the relatively prosperous Ivory Coast, a significant incursion by Japan into Francophone Africa.

In stark contrast, the United States failed to increase its share of the market in a statistically significant manner in any one of the groupings used in this study. In Black Africa excluding Nigeria it recorded a statistically significant decline in market shares. Perhaps more serious was a similar statistically significant drop in its share in the expanding Nigerian market—worrisome especially because the United States is Nigeria's single most important customer for its oil exports. The over $10 billion that the United States pays annually for Nigerian oil is the major component in its unfavorable balance of trade with the region. In the case of South Africa, the other significant trading partner in the region for Japan as well as the United States, both Japan and the United States maintained an approximate equilibrium in balance of trade over the last decade.

Whereas the United States was registering record balance-of-trade deficits with Africa by the end of the 1970s, Japan was recording unprecedented surpluses—in large part as a result of its increased sales to Nigeria. Black Africa's surplus on trade with the United States has enabled it to run continuous trade deficits with its other principal trading partners—Japan, the EC, and the OPEC countries.

Only the most narrow of mercantilist approaches would require trade to be balanced on a regional basis. Divergent experiences in trade balances with Africa over the last decade reflect the lack of symmetry between the Japanese and U.S. economies and the pursuit of different national foreign economic policies. Geographical factors, combined with the local availability of raw materials, may make it advantageous for Japan to import oil from the Middle East and Southeast Asia rather than from West Africa. Accordingly, the fact that the United States is running a large balance-of-trade deficit with Africa while Japan enjoys a trade surplus may or may not be perceived as a significant problem by U.S. decision-makers. At the same time, however, there are areas of economic activity in Africa where Japanese and U.S. interests are in direct competition—particularly in the search for new markets for exports of manufactured goods. In order to better understand the nature of this competition, we undertook a detailed analysis of the changing composition of Japanese and U.S. exports to the continent over the last decade (Chapter 2).

For Japan the most prominent change in the composition of its exports to Africa over the 1970s has been a growth in the relative importance of machinery and transport equipment. Exports in this category have grown more rapidly than those of manufactured goods. Two factors might be important in this context. First, a permissive factor: the market in Black Africa for capital goods has grown rapidly as countries have actively pursued policies of import substitution. Second, there has been a sustained effort by Japanese manufacturers to upgrade their exports toward goods which incorporate a higher domestic value-added. This is in accord with the structural changes (noted in Chapter 3) which have occurred in the Japanese economy over the last fifteen years. For instance, whereas in the early 1970s textiles had a prominent role in Japanese exports to Africa, in the second half of the decade exports of textile machinery had assumed some importance.

For the United States the most significant change in the composition of exports was an increased share of food, beverages, and tobacco. Although this might be perceived, quite correctly, as an area in which the United States enjoys a comparative advantage over Japan, any enthusiasm regarding increased U.S. exports in these categories must be tempered by the knowledge that a significant proportion of their value was financed by U.S. foreign aid. In 1980, for example, total aid to Africa and the Food for Peace Program amounted to 30 percent of the value of U.S. food exports to the region; one half of this aid was in grant form. If it had not been for the growth in food aid to the continent, the U.S. share of African markets would have declined even more precipitously than we observed.

U.S. exporters have not kept pace with their Japanese competitors in the important category of machinery and transport equipment sales. Considering that the United States has already relinquished a significant part of its domestic market in radios, T.V.s, tape recorders, and—perhaps most important—automobiles to Japanese products, it is hardly surprising that Japan has outperformed the United States in sales of these consumer goods to Africa. Of greater concern is Japan's relative success in increasing its share of the African market for capital equipment. Although the dollar value of U.S. exports of capital equipment to Africa continues to exceed that of the Japanese, Japan has overtaken the United States in exports of metal-working equipment and telecommunications machinery and is rapidly catching up in the sales of internal combustion equipment and heavy electrical machinery. In some areas the United States continues to hold a substantial advantage—office machines and heating, cooling, and cargo-handling machinery—suggesting that Japan's competitive success up to now has been sectorally specific.[1]

Not only have Japan's exports of machinery and transport equipment grown rapidly for Africa in general, but also Japan has enjoyed considerable success in penetrating the markets of Black Africa in particular. Black Africa accounted in 1980 for 70 percent of Japan's sales of telecommunications and heavy electrical equipment. In contrast, over half of U.S. sales of goods in this category in 1980 went to the South African market. It appears that the United States is in danger of missing out on the expanding markets for

111

capital goods in Black Africa. This is particularly the case in Nigeria, where Japanese corporations outsold their American competitors by a ratio of more than three to one in 1980. Although the South African market remains of importance, it would be shortsighted on the part of U.S. industry to focus on it at the expense of diversifying markets in the rest of the continent.

In the Black African market political factors may also come into play. One of the few means available to African countries to attempt to influence U.S. policy is to threaten to exclude U.S. firms from their markets. The Reagan Administration's policies toward South Africa have won the United States few friends in Black Africa. It is quite possible that a continuation of the policy of accommodation toward South Africa will provoke some African countries into a boycott of U.S. goods and the exclusion of U.S. firms from construction projects in their countries.

Africa has had a growing share of Japanese aid and investment over the 1970s. As noted, at the end of the 1960s Japan's aid efforts were concentrated almost exclusively on Asia. In the following decade, Africa's share of total Japanese aid increased from negligible proportions to approximately 10 percent—roughly equal to its share in total U.S. aid. A number of factors explain this increase: Japan's interest in promoting resource projects in order to diversify its sources of raw materials, a development of markets particularly for Japanese capital goods exports, Tokyo's desire to respond to Third World criticism that its aid was excessively concentrated in geographical terms and that insufficient efforts were being made to assist the least developed countries, an increased concern for basic human needs, and an increasing Japanese concern regarding geopolitical factors, particularly the expanding Soviet presence in the Indian Ocean area.

Africa's share in Japanese overseas investment has also increased over the 1970s, whereas the reverse is true of its share in U.S. overseas investment. However, sub-Saharan Africa still accounts for less than 2 percent of total Japanese overseas investment. Contrary to popular impressions, the single most important locus for Japanese investment has not been resource projects, but shipping firms in Liberia (many of which remain under 100 percent Japanese ownership). Over the past decade, Japanese corporations have invested in light manufacturing and assembly plants to supply local African markets. Notable among these investments are textile plants and assembly plants for transportation equipment in Nigeria and electrical appliances in Kenya. Textile plants have also been built in Ethiopia, Kenya, Mauritius, Sudan, and Tanzania. Demands from these plants have contributed to the growing importance of capital equipment in the composition of Japan's exports to Africa.

Although mining has been a major growth area for Japan in recent years, at present there are only eleven mineral projects in operation in Africa. Our interviews with Japanese decision-makers lead us to believe that Black Africa will not grow in importance in this aspect of Japan's overseas investments. While Japan was willing in the early 1970s—a time of great concern regarding future supplies of raw materials—to undertake investments that were perceived by others as being too risky (e.g., copper mining in Zaire's Shaba Province), the current prevailing orthodoxy in Tokyo is that the risk of African mineral ventures generally has not been worthwhile (with the exception of uranium in Niger and oil in Gabon). Having successfully diversified its sources of raw materials over the last decade, Japan is now much more discriminating in choosing new projects and places greater emphasis on the potential reliability of new suppliers. Black Africa does not score highly on this count. South Africa is the principal source of Japanese imports of minerals and agricultural products from the region.

If one aspect of Japanese economic activity in Africa must be singled out which might cause alarm to U.S. policymakers, it is the relative success of Japanese corporations in winning a growing share of the market for capital equipment in Black Africa. It is impossible for us to isolate the reasons for the differences in performance— whether, for instance, it comes from the superiority of the technology offered by Japan, or competitive pricing policy, or a greater effort by Japanese entrepreneurs to penetrate new and often difficult markets. Pauline Baker notes that there is a reluctance on the part of U.S. industry to take the risks which are perceived to be involved in Africa. In addition, U.S. corporations tend to adopt a short time-horizon on investments which places them at a disadvantage, especially vis-à-vis their Japanese competitors.[2]

In addition to the characteristics of business decision-making, on which governments can have only a minor impact, there are certain structural features of the Japanese economy which provide an advantage to Japanese corporations which would be difficult for U.S.

corporations to match—e.g., the role of the sogo shosha in promoting international commerce. At the same time, we have identified a number of government policies which influence overseas activities; it is clear that the Japanese government provides more support to its private sector abroad than does the U.S. government. Such policies need to be considered most carefully by U.S. policymakers in deciding how the Japanese challenge in the Third World may best be met.

African markets offer particularly difficult business climates for corporations from any country. As noted in Chapter 3, Japanese executives perceive the same problems in doing business with Africa as do their U.S. competitors. Yet despite these difficulties, which in the Japanese case are compounded by a lack of familiarity with African markets, language, and cultural differences, Japanese industry has outperformed its U.S. counterpart in the 1970s. In an uncertain business environment like that of Africa, governments can play a major role in reducing the risks borne by the private sector. Our review of government policies in Chapter 5 demonstrated that the Japanese private sector is the beneficiary of programs which are both quantitatively and qualitatively superior to those provided by the U.S. government to its private sector. Japan's EXIM Bank, for instance, offers a much wider range of programs than its U.S. equivalent. Particularly important is its provision of mixed credits—a combination of export credits and concessional loans—and its willingness to contribute to the local costs of a project. Mixed credits, which are also offered by most West European export credit agencies, are of great significance in the markets of the poorest developing countries, where commercial credit rates frequently are too high for local purchasers. Similarly, assistance with the local costs of major projects may be essential in countries which have critical shortages of capital. Willingness to provide mixed credits and local cost supports surely contributed to the success of Japanese corporations in winning contracts for major resource projects in Africa in the last decade.

Since it has been unable to offer mixed credits, the U.S. EXIM has had to be more conservative in its evaluation of projects. As a result, it has been unwilling over the years to finance infrastructural and import-substituting projects—two major growth areas in Black Africa. Already at a disadvantage, the U.S. EXIM has been further handicapped by high U.S. domestic interest rates. Japan, despite its willingness to provide mixed credits and local cost supports, has abided by the guidelines laid down by the OECD regarding export credit subsidies. Unlike some of its European counterparts, the Japanese EXIM has not undercut its U.S. competitor by cheating on interest rates. In fact, by respecting the OECD guidelines, Japan's EXIM has placed its exporters in a worse position than would otherwise be the case since they are now required to offer export credits at interest rates exceeding those in the domestic economy. Rather than cheating on the part of the Japanese, it has been the high interest rates within the U.S. economy which have made the U.S. export credit program uncompetitive.

The U.S. EXIM's position has been further undermined by recent administration cutbacks to its funding. OPIC, whose insurance policies match those of MITI (although at higher cost to the purchaser), has similarly come under Congressional attack. Given the Reagan Administration's emphasis on the private sector, it is quite perverse that these institutions have been starved of funds.[3] Both EXIM and OPIC have very successfully promoted U.S. business overseas at a minimal cost to the U.S. taxpayer.

Regardless of the wishful thinking in certain conservative quarters of the United States, it is impossible to remove governments from contemporary international trade. Most African countries have very small domestic private sectors; accordingly, many projects offering opportunities to U.S. exporters are managed by government departments or parastatals. These agencies naturally expect that the home government of a corporation bidding for a contract will be involved in piecing together a comprehensive package of public and private finance. By preventing the U.S. EXIM from offering a competitive package of support to U.S. corporations, the administration is merely ensuring that U.S. interests in many cases will be excluded from consideration in the award of major contracts. To be sure, cut-throat competition among exporting countries in offering subsidized credits is shortsighted and liable to provoke further erosion of the liberal trading order. However, such damaging activities have increasingly been recognized and considerable progress has been made in recent years in reconstituting the "gentleman's agreement" in the OECD which provides a viable regime for the international oversight of export credits. If the U.S. government opts out of providing support for the overseas operations of its private sector, it will merely be tying its own hands.

A failure by the U.S. government to support the operations of U.S. corporations abroad through a competitive program of export credits and investment insurance will further reinforce the perceptions frequently held by U.S. business that the relationship with government is an adversary one rather than a mutually supportive partnership. There are two principal areas where U.S. corporations perceive that government polices handicap their overseas operations: anti-trust legislation and the Foreign Corrupt Practices Act. Anti-trust legislation makes it more difficult for U.S. corporations to enter into the type of trading combines which have been so successful in promoting Japanese exports. Recent legislation before Congress has attempted to remove some of the difficulties; as yet, it is too early to determine how successful this will be.

Although the intention of the Foreign Corrupt Practices Act is a worthy one, the fact that restrictions against improper practices have been imposed only by the U.S. government on U.S. corporations handicaps them in their competition with European and Japanese exporters. As in the case of the trade war in subsidized export credits, competition in bribing foreign officials is undesirable for all exporting countries. But a solution to this dubious practice cannot be found in the unilateral action of one government, however well-meaning the intention, because this action will merely place its own exporters at a disadvantage and may, perversely, encourage others to expand their corrupt practices.[4] As in the case of export credit subsidies, the solution should lie in the negotiation of an international arrangement. Again, the OECD is the logical choice for overseeing such arrangements.

In addition to reducing the risk of overseas operations, governments have a major role to play in increasing the knowledge of their domestic corporations about the foreign markets available. In this area as well, the United States lags behind Japan. Government sources of information are particularly important for the small- and medium-sized firms. (Major transnationals typically have their own intelligence networks.) In the United States the role of the government is even more important than in Japan since smaller U.S. enterprises do not have any equivalent of the soga shosha on which to depend for information. Part of the problem in penetrating the African market for U.S. business is simply a lack of knowledge. Impressions gained from the press regarding the business climate and political instability of

African countries may be far from accurate. Business representatives who have participated in Department of Commerce missions to various African countries generally have reported pleasant surprise at the opportunities available.

Clearly at present the U.S. Foreign Commercial Service is not providing adequate support in Africa. However, as in the case of the U.S. EXIM and OPIC, it is ironic that its activities have been curtailed by budgetary difficulties. Much more can and should be done to provide U.S. business with more information on overseas opportunities. OPIC's "Opportunity Bank"—a computerized data system that can match potential investors with venture capital opportunities in developing countries—is a step in the right direction (and negates some of the advantages provided to European companies through their own commercial services and the Center for Industrial Development established as part of the Lomé Conventions).

In our analysis of foreign aid in Chapter 4 we noted that despite recent Japanese efforts to diversify the types of assistance given, and in particular to pay more attention to meeting basic human needs, Japan has primarily provided support for infrastructure and mining and construction projects. Accordingly, most aid to Africa has been given to countries where Japan has an interest in resource projects. Although most Japanese aid has now been untied (at least with respect to procurement from developing countries), the involvement of the Japanese private sector in identifying and proposing projects to the government serves to ensure that a large proportion of aid contracts is awarded to Japanese industries. Moreover, Japan's aid continues to be given on terms that are less generous than the norm for OECD donors.

In contrast, a much larger percentage of U.S. aid in recent years has been devoted to areas concerned with the fulfillment of basic human needs—agriculture, education, health, and welfare. Especially in the light of Japan's generally superior export record in Africa, the contrast might appear to suggest that the United States should abandon its focus on meeting basic human needs and concentrate solely on projects which are designed to promote the interests of the U.S. private sector. We do not draw this conclusion from our analysis for two major reasons. First, U.S. food aid, while of major benefit to African recipients, has also assisted the U.S. domestic agricultural sector by disposing of surplus food stocks. Second, as a superpower, the United States has interests in Africa which sometimes differ from those of other countries. Long-term U.S. interests on the continent are affected by the general image that the U.S. government enjoys, and in part they are well served by maintaining the goodwill of African governments. Provision of support for humanitarian objectives has over the years been a major source of goodwill for the United States.

While we argue strongly for additional government support for the U.S. private sector's operations overseas, we emphasize that such support should be effected primarily through such specialized agencies as EXIM and OPIC. In addition, packages to assist U.S. exporters can be made more competitive by supplementing export credits with concessional finance, but increased support of the private sector should not come at the expense of traditional aid programs; both policy tools are important for furthering U.S. objectives in Africa.

Appendices

A. NONPARAMETRIC TESTS

B. AFRICAN COUNTRY GROUPINGS

C. BALANCE-OF-TRADE TABLES

D. INVESTMENT TABLES FOR THE UNITED STATES

E. U.S. AID TO AFRICA

NONPARAMETRIC TESTS

To examine changes in trade patterns between selected groupings of African countries and one or more of their trading partners, we shall consider the total exports and imports of the African grouping to and from its trading partners six years before and six years after 1976. More precisely, we shall try to determine whether the levels of exports and imports for 1976-81 are different from those for 1970-75.

Because of a worldwide inflationary trend during the 1970s, both exports and imports display an upward trend throughout each of the sample periods considered (when expressed in monetary units). In order to neutralize the effect of inflation, for any given year we divide the exports or imports to or from an African grouping by the exports or imports to or from the entire world. We call these ratios export and import "shares," as they represent the African grouping's share of world trade.

Our objective is to detect whether there has been any change in the average export/import shares in the two sample periods. Against our null hypothesis (that no statistically significant change in market shares occurred), we test two alternative hypotheses: (a) that market shares increased; and (b) that market shares declined. An alternative hypothesis is accepted where there is a 95 percent probability that market shares either increased or declined. Any test of these two hypotheses is subject to the following types of errors:

1. *Type I error*: Rejection of the null hypothesis when in fact it is true. (In Chapter 2, type I error is referred to by the more common concept of statistical significance.)
2. *Type II error*: Acceptance of the null hypothesis when in fact it is false.

The choice of a test for the null hypothesis should be made with a criterion to keep both types of errors as small as possible. In reality it

119

is impossible to minimize type I and II errors simultaneously. Thus we chose to keep the level of type I error fixed at 5 percent. The modest sample size (two times six years) does not warrant a parametric test to prove or reject the two hypotheses. Instead we take recourse to a more robust nonparametric test particularly suited for this type of problem, the Wilcoxon-Mann-Whitney (W) test, that minimizes errors of type II.

COMPARISON OF W-TESTS WITH t-TESTS

W- and t-tests have one assumption in common—i.e., that the two underlying populations from which the samples are drawn are identical except for possible differences in their means. The t-test makes the additional assumption that the underlying populations are normal.

The t-test is the "best" test when the underlying populations indeed are normal. By "best" we mean that it is the test with lowest type II error when type I error is fixed. The W-test, however, compares well with the t-test in relative efficiency—that is, in the ratio of sample sizes required to give equal probabilities of type I and type II errors. In fact, when the underlying population is not normal, the W-test actually surpasses the t-test in efficiency. An additional advantage offered by the W-test is that it does not give undue emphasis to "outliers" resulting from imperfect data collection. This property is relevant to our analysis, as indicated by the frequent corrections that the IMF directions of trade data are subject to. For these reasons we chose to use the W-test.

EXAMPLE OF THE W-TEST

As an illustration of the W-test, let us examine the data in Table A-1, which were used to examine changes in Japan's share in the exports of Africa (excluding Nigeria).

The shares of Africa's (excluding Nigeria's) exports to Japan as a percentage of such exports to the world were calculated and ranked, with the lowest ranking equal to 1 and the highest equal to 12. A decline of Japan's export shares is particularly striking: from a level

Table A-1

EXPORTS FROM AFRICA (EXCLUDING NIGERIA) TO JAPAN, 1970-81

Export Property	1970	1971	1972	1973	1974	1975	1976	1977	1978	1979	1980	1981
Size *(Millions of dollars)*	702	666	797	1068	1316	1253	1282	1421	1497	2048	2608	2762
Share *(Percent)*	8.29	8.35	8.52	8.45	7.52	5.99	5.80	5.38	5.17	5.25	5.22	5.85
Growth *(Percent)*	11.7	-5.0	19.7	33.9	23.3	-4.8	2.3	10.8	5.4	36.8	27.3	5.9
Ranks	9	10	12	11	8	7	5	4	1	3	2	6
Statistics			Rank 1970-75 = 57						Rank 1976-81 = 21			

Source: Export volumes to the EC and to the world were obtained from IMF, *Direction of Trade Statistics Yearbook*, 1976, 1980, and 1982.

121

in the 8 percent range before 1975, the export shares are consistently in the 5 percent range after 1975.

For the export shares application, the W-test statistic is the sum of the 1970-75 ranks. Very high or very low values of the W-test statistic are grounds to reject the null hypothesis. For two samples of six each, the highest W value is 57, the lowest is 21. In Table A-1 the sum of the ranks from 1970 to 1975 is 57. (The sum of 1976-81 ranks is given for clarity; it provides no new information.) The Wilcoxon-Mann-Whitney tests show that by rejecting the null hypothesis that export shares remained unchanged, we risk a (type I) error with less than 0.1 percent probability. In general, we do not require such a stringent criterion for type I errors. We require only that the probability of type I errors be less than or equal to 5 percent (i.e., a significance level of 5 percent or less) in order to reject the null hypothesis.

Appendix B

AFRICAN COUNTRY GROUPINGS

Table B-1

AFRICAN COUNTRIES IN OUR SAMPLE

Angola	Guinea	Sao Tome and Principe
Benin	Guinea Bissau	Senegal
Botswana	Ivory Coast	Seychelles
Burundi	Kenya	Sierra Leone
Cameroon	Lesotho	Somalia
Cape Verde	Liberia	South Africa
Central African Republic	Madagascar	Sudan
Chad	Malawi	Swaziland
Comoros	Mali	Tanzania
Congo	Mauritania	Togo
Djibouti	Mauritius	Uganda
Equatorial Guinea	Mozambique	Upper Volta
Ethiopia	Niger	Zaire
Gabon	Nigeria	Zambia
Gambia	Rwanda	Zimbabwe
Ghana		

Table B-2

AFRICAN COUNTRY GROUPINGS FOR NONPARAMETRIC TESTS

Commonwealth Africa

Botswana	Malawi	Swaziland
Gambia	Mauritius	Tanzania
Ghana	Nigeria	Uganda
Kenya	Sierra Leone	Zambia
Lesotho		

East Africa

Kenya	Tanzania	Uganda

Francophone Africa

Benin	Gabon	Rwanda
Burundi	Ivory Coast	Senegal
Cameroon	Madagascar	Somalia[a]
Central African Republic	Mali	Togo
Chad	Mauritania	Upper Volta
Congo	Niger	Zaire

Least Developed Africa

Benin	Gambia	Sao Tome and Principe
Botswana	Guinea	Seychelles
Burundi	Guinea Bissau	Somalia
Cape Verde	Lesotho	Sudan
Central African Republic	Malawi	Swaziland
Chad	Mali	Tanzania
Comoros	Mauritania	Togo
Djibouti	Niger	Uganda
Ethiopia	Rwanda	Upper Volta

Non-Oil Francophone Africa

Benin	Madagascar	Senegal
Burundi	Mali	Somalia[a]
Cameroon	Mauritania	Togo
Central African Republic	Niger	Upper Volta
Chad	Rwanda	Zaire
Ivory Coast		

Oil Africa

Angola	Gabon	Nigeria
Congo		

[a]Somalia was included in these groupings because, although not a Francophone country, it enjoyed preferential arrangements with the EC under the Yaoundé Conventions.

Appendix C

BALANCE-OF-TRADE TABLES

Table C-1

JAPANESE AND U.S. BALANCE OF TRADE WITH AFRICA, 1970-81[a]
(Billions of dollars)

Year	Japan	United States
1970	$ -0.27[b]	$ 0.09
1971	0.01	0.10
1972	-0.19	-0.24
1973	-0.32	-0.59
1974	-0.29	-3.36
1975	0.19	-3.47
1976	0.27	-5.85
1977	0.90	-7.86
1978	0.92	-7.13
1979	-0.14	-11.45
1980	1.22	-13.87
1981	2.26	-10.38

Source: IMF, *Direction of Trade Statistics Yearbook*, 1972, 1976, 1982.

[a]Balance of trade is calculated as exports minus imports.

[b]A minus sign indicates a deficit.

Table C-2

JAPANESE AND U.S. BALANCE OF TRADE WITH AFRICA EXCLUDING NIGERIA, 1970-81
(Billions of dollars)

Year	Japan	United States
1970	$ -0.32[a]	$ 0.04
1971	-0.06	0.02
1972	-0.24	-0.07
1973	-0.28	-0.06
1974	-1.12	-0.64
1975	-0.12	-0.84
1976	-0.20	-1.35
1977	-0.10	-1.71
1978	-0.01	-1.58
1979	-0.90	-1.88
1980	-0.16	-2.53
1981	0.45	-2.71

Source: Same as Table C-1.

Table C-3

AFRICA'S BALANCE OF TRADE WITH ITS MAJOR TRADING PARTNERS, 1970-81
(Billions of dollars)

Year	Japan	United States	EC	OPEC[a]
1970	$ -0.16	$ -0.36	$ -0.20	$ -0.12
1971	-0.30	-0.36	-0.12	-0.12
1972	-0.51	0.99	-0.22	-0.10
1973	-0.27	0.36	0.15	-0.15
1974	-0.27	1.83	2.61	-0.75
1975	-0.64	1.18	-2.02	-0.93
1976	-0.84	2.83	-1.10	-0.83
1977	-1.47	4.33	-2.43	-0.67
1978	-1.99	6.33	-5.30	-0.44
1979	-0.77	8.84	-0.75	-0.76
1980	-2.06	10.40	-3.89	-1.08
1981	-3.00	8.10	-10.40	-1.44

Source: Same as Table C-1.

[a]Nigeria is excluded from the OPEC figures.

Table C-4

BALANCE OF TRADE OF AFRICA EXCLUDING NIGERIA WITH AFRICA'S MAJOR TRADING PARTNERS, 1970-81
(Billions of dollars)

Year	Japan	United States	EC	OPEC
1970	$ 0.04	$ -0.35	$ 0.20	$ -0.12
1971	-0.20	-0.47	-1.49	-0.12
1972	0.01	-0.31	-0.61	-0.11
1973	-0.01	-0.29	-0.53	-0.15
1974	-0.40	-0.35	-0.44	-0.74
1975	-0.33	-0.47	-2.11	-0.92
1976	-0.13	-0.33	-0.11	-0.83
1977	-0.31	0.88	0.16	-0.67
1978	-0.63	1.49	-2.16	-0.44
1979	0.07	1.44	-1.39	-0.75
1980	-0.52	1.23	-4.55	-1.07
1981	-0.94	1.09	-6.09	-1.43

Source: Same as Table C-1.

NOTE: Figures in Tables C-3 and C-4 for the Japanese and U.S. trade balances with Africa are not identical to those in Tables C-1 and C-2 because they are calculated from the perspective of African countries—i.e., they reflect insurance and freight charges for African imports. Delays in shipping and recording transactions also cause discrepancies between data on Japanese and U.S. imports and exports for a given period and those for African imports and exports for the same period.

INVESTMENT TABLES FOR THE UNITED STATES

Table D-1

GROWTH OF TOTAL U.S. FOREIGN DIRECT INVESTMENT, 1966-78

Year	Total (Millions of dollars)	Increment (Millions of dollars)	Growth Rate (Percent)
1966	$ 51,792	—	—
1967	56,560	$ 4,768	9.2%
1968	61,907	5,347	9.4
1969	68,093	6,186	10.0
1970	75,480	7,387	10.8
1971	82,760	7,280	9.6
1972	89,878	7,118	8.6
1973	101,313	11,435	12.7
1974	110,078	8,765	8.6
1975	124,050	13,972	12.7
1976	136,809	12,759	10.3
1977	149,848	13,039	9.5
1978	168,081	18,233	12.2

Source: U.S. Department of Commerce, "Selected Data on U.S. Direct Investment Abroad," 1966-1978.

Table D-2

GROWTH OF U.S. FOREIGN DIRECT INVESTMENT IN DEVELOPING COUNTRIES, 1966-78

Year	Total (Millions of dollars)	Increment (Millions of dollars)	Growth Rate (Percent)
1966	$ 13,866	—	—
1967	14,905	$ 1,039	7.5%
1968	16,497	1,592	10.7
1969	17,627	1,130	6.8
1970	19,192	1,565	8.9
1971	20,719	1,527	7.9
1972	22,274	1,555	7.5
1973	22,904	630	2.8
1974	19,848	−3,056	−13.3
1975	26,288	6,440	32.4
1976	29,313	3,025	11.5
1977	34,462	5,151	17.6
1978	40,466	6,004	17.4

Source: Same as Table D-1.

Table D-3

GROWTH OF U.S. FOREIGN DIRECT INVESTMENT IN AFRICA, 1966-78[a]

Year	Total *(Millions of dollars)*	Increment *(Millions of dollars)*	Growth Rate *(Percent)*
1966	$ 1,344	—	—
1967	1,492	$ 148	11.0%
1968	1,807	315	21.1
1969	2,031	224	12.4
1970	2,427	396	19.5
1971	2,644	217	8.9
1972	2,835	191	7.2
1973	2,376	−459	−16.2
1974	2,233	−143	−6.0
1975	2,414	181	8.1
1976	2,775	361	14.9
1977	2,802	27	0.9
1978	3,411	609	21.7

Source: Same as Table D-1.

[a]Africa includes north Africa but excludes South Africa.

Table D-4

GROWTH OF U.S. FOREIGN DIRECT INVESTMENT IN
SOUTH AFRICA, 1966-78

Year	Total *(Millions of dollars)*	Increment *(Millions of dollars)*	Growth Rate *(Percent)*
1966	$ 490	—	—
1967	556	$ 66	13.5%
1968	616	60	10.8
1969	672	56	9.1
1970	778	106	15.8
1971	875	97	12.5
1972	941	66	7.5
1973	1,167	226	24.0
1974	1,463	296	25.4
1975	1,582	119	8.1
1976	1,668	86	5.4
1977	1,792	124	7.4
1978	1,994	202	11.3

Source: Same as Table D-1.

Table D-5

AFRICA'S SHARE IN U.S. FOREIGN DIRECT INVESTMENT (FDI), 1966-78[a]
(Percent)

Year	Investment in South Africa as Share of Cumulative Total U.S. FDI	Investment in Africa as Share of Cumulative Total U.S. FDI	Investment in Africa as Share of Total U.S. FDI in Developing Countries
1966	0.94%	2.59%	9.69%
1967	0.98	2.63	10.01
1968	0.99	2.91	10.95
1969	0.98	2.98	11.52
1970	1.03	3.21	12.64
1971	1.05	3.19	12.76
1972	1.04	3.15	12.72
1973	1.15	2.34	10.37
1974	1.32	2.02	11.25
1975	1.27	1.94	9.18
1976	1.21	2.02	9.46
1977	1.19	1.86	8.13
1978	1.18	2.02	8.42

Source: Same as Table D-1.

[a]Africa includes north Africa but excludes South Africa.

Table D-6

DISTRIBUTION OF U.S. FOREIGN DIRECT INVESTMENT IN AFRICA BY SECTOR, 1978

(Percent)

Country or Area	Mining and Smelting	Petroleum	Manufacturing	Sector Transport, Communications, Public Utilities	Trade	Finance, Insurance	Other
South Africa	N.A.[b]	N.A.	37.3%[c]	0.1%	11.5%	N.A.	4.3%
Other Africa[a]	16.0%	61.3%	8.0[d]	2.6	4.4	2.2%	5.5

Source: Calculated from data in U.S. Department of Commerce, "Selected Data on U.S. Investment Abroad," 1966-1978.

[a]Includes Algeria, Libya, Morocco, and Tunisia.

[b]The Department of Commerce withholds data in cases where publication would identify the holdings of an individual U.S. firm.

[c]Constituents include chemical products (6.16 percent), primary fabricated materials (2.78 percent), and machinery (8.82 percent).

[d]Constituents include food products (0.8 percent), chemical products (1.64 percent), and machinery (0.32 percent).

Appendix E

U.S. AID TO AFRICA

Table E-1

BLACK AFRICA'S SHARE IN U.S. AID, 1962-82
(Percent)

Type of Aid	Average, 1962-78	1979	1980	1981	1982
Total Economic Assistance	6.1%	7.6%	9.8%	11.3%	10.8%
Loans	5.0	5.9	8.6	13.2	11.0
Grants	6.8	8.2	10.2	10.9	10.7
Food for Peace	5.9	14.3	20.5	20.8	15.8
Loans	3.3	10.8	16.3	18.8	17.8
Grants	8.9	19.2	26.4	22.8	13.6
Total Military Assistance	1.0	0.4	3.7	2.6	4.6
Loans	2.3	0.5	5.1	3.1	3.3
Grants	0.6	0.2	0.4	1.0	8.0
EXIM Bank Loans	3.5	15.7	3.7	8.9	7.2

Source: USAID, *U.S. Overseas Loans and Grants and Assistance from International Organizations* [CONG-R-0105] (Washington, D.C.: Government Printing Office, 1983).

131

Table E-2

U.S. AID TO AFRICA BY COUNTRY, 1946-82

(*Millions of dollars*)

Country	Total Economic Assistance		Food for Peace		Total Military Assistance		EXIM Bank Loans	
	Loans	Grants	Loans	Grants	Loans	Grants	Gross	Net[a]
Angola	–	$ 15.1	–	$ 15.1	–	–	$ 99.6	$ 68.4
Benin (Dahomey)	$ 23.7	34.4	–	12.6	–	$ 0.1	0.2	–
Botswana	16.7	135.4	–	56.6	$ 1.0	0.2	–	–
Burundi	–	38.0	–	23.7	–	–	–	–
Cameroon	29.3	83.6	–	13.1	13.9	0.4	152.9	113.5
Cape Verde	3.0	46.9	–	21.6	–	–	–	–
Central African Republic	–	20.3	–	4.5	–	–	2.8	2.4
Chad	–	71.4	–	35.0	–	–	–	–
Comoros	–	1.4	–	1.4	–	–	–	–
Congo, Republic of	1.9	14.2	$ 1.9	9.2	–	–	7.0	6.0
Djibouti	–	13.8	–	5.2	–	0.1	–	–
Entente States[b]	33.7	4.6	–	–	–	–	–	–
Equatorial Guinea	–	2.3	–	0.3	–	–	–	–
Ethiopia	143.2	251.8	9.6	90.2	36.0	244.2	41.6	5.5
Gabon	–	14.7	–	0.8	11.2	0.2	23.7	0.9
Gambia	–	33.5	–	13.7	–	–	–	–
Ghana	274.9	157.7	100.4	62.2	–	1.8	127.4	48.3
Guinea	101.0	76.5	93.4	–	–	1.0	28.4	0.2
Guinea-Bissau	–	26.3	–	14.4	–	–	–	–

Table E-2 (cont.)

Country	Total Economic Assistance		Food for Peace		Total Military Assistance		EXIM Bank Loans	
	Loans	Grants	Loans	Grants	Loans	Grants	Gross	Net[a]
Ivory Coast	$ 14.3	$ 33.3	$ 7.4	$ 7.5	–	$ 0.3	$345.1	$246.4
Kenya	157.9	235.0	58.1	44.1	$135.0	14.3	18.9	1.8
Lesotho	–	120.4	–	65.1	–	–	–	–
Liberia	149.2	280.8	40.1	9.8	22.9	17.0	115.3	-57.1
Madagascar	14.5	27.9	9.5	22.7	–	0.1	1.8	–
Malawi	33.1	49.3	2.2	5.3	–	3.5	–	–
Mali	6.8	166.5	0.4	50.0	–	0.1	–	3.5
Mauritania	1.4	86.6	–	44.5	–	–	5.9	–
Mauritius	12.0	22.8	12.0	18.8	–	–	–	8.6
Mozambique	14.0	52.3	14.0	40.8	–	–	35.9	4.0
Niger	3.5	150.9	–	–	4.3	0.7	5.4	–
Nigeria	83.6	322.9	–	67.0	0.3	1.5	416.0	372.1
Rwanda	–	46.1	–	22.0	1.5	0.1	–	–
Sao Tome and Principe	–	2.4	–	0.5	–	–	–	–
Senegal	8.6	195.3	8.6	80.3	8.0	3.8	7.7	0.8
Seychelles	–	6.7	–	2.1	–	–	–	–
Sierra Leone	13.0	88.9	13.0	25.0	–	–	28.8	11.2
Somalia	82.8	230.5	66.8	100.7	50.0	15.8	–	–
South Africa	1.3	–	–	–	–	–	149.3	-34.1
Sudan	102.6	390.0	78.8	35.0	111.3	55.2	5.9	-1.3
Swaziland	10.8	54.3	–	7.0	–	–	–	–
Tanzania	88.3	240.4	46.2	103.4	–	–	15.7	10.7

Table E-2 (cont.)

Country	Total Economic Assistance		Food for Peace		Total Military Assistance		EXIM Bank Loans	
	Loans	Grants	Loans	Grants	Loans	Grants	Gross	Net[a]
Togo	–	$ 67.3	–	$ 25.7	–	$ 0.1	$ 1.4	$ -0.9
Uganda	$ 11.4	58.5	–	16.8	–	0.1	–	–
Upper Volta	–	188.9	–	92.3	–	0.5	1.0	0.2
Zaire	333.7	368.3	$194.3	88.7	$130.6	43.1	223.0	137.6
Zambia	205.5	34.4	53.9	14.2	–	–	100.0	14.4
Zimbabwe	5.0	127.7	–	2.8	–	0.1	39.4	38.4
Portuguese territories	–	3.4	–	0.2	–	–	–	–
Central and West Africa[c]	–	169.8	–	0.4	–	–	–	–
East Africa[d]	2.6	30.7	2.6	–	–	–	–	–
Southern African region	17.3	108.0	–	–	–	–	–	–
Africa regional	67.4	504.2	–	1.2	–	–	–	–
GRAND TOTAL	2068.1	5506.4	813.2	1373.5	526.1	404.1	2000.3	904.9

Source: Same as Table E-1.

[a]Total loans and grants less repayments and interest.
[b]Conseil de l'Entente: Benin, Ivory Coast, Niger, Togo, and Upper Volta.
[c]Regional.
[d]Regional.

NOTES

Chapter 1

1. Figures from Japan, Ministry of International Trade and Industry (MITI), *Economic Cooperation of Japan, 1981* (Tokyo, July 1982), p. 13.

2. Sunday O. Agbi, *Japan's Attitudes and Policies Towards African Issues Since 1945: A Historical Perspective* (Tokyo: Institute of Developing Economies, 1982).

3. This aspect of the "free rider" problem is explored in detail in Robert Rothstein, *Global Bargaining* (Princeton: Princeton University Press, 1979). A more sympathetic but not particularly convincing account of Japan's role in North-South negotiations is given by Shigeko N. Fukai, "Japan's North-South Dialogue at the United Nations," *World Politics* 35, 1 (October 1982): 73-105.

4. Chester A. Crocker, "African Policy in the 1980s," *Washington Quarterly* 3, 3 (Summer 1980): 77.

Chapter 3

1. Terutomo Ozawa, *Multinationalism, Japanese Style* (Princeton University Press, 1979).

2. *Ibid.*

3. Hugh Patrick and Henry Rosovsky, *Asia's New Giant: How the Japanese Economy Works* (Washington, D.C.: Brookings Institution, 1976), p. 389.

4. *The Role of Trading Companies in International Commerce* (JETRO Marketing Series 2, Tokyo, revised 1982).

5. Alexander K. Young, *The Sogo Shosha: Japan's Multinational Trading Companies* (Boulder, Colo.: Westview Press, 1979), p. 58.

6. Chiyoura Masamichi, "Investment Activities in Africa by Japanese Companies," *Economic Studies Institute Journal* (University of Dokyo, Soka, Japan, 1977).

7. For a study of Japan's success in diversifying its sources of supply, see Dani Rodrik, "Managing Resource Dependency: The United States and Japan in the Markets for Copper, Iron Ore and Bauxite," *World Development* 10, 7 (July 1982): 541-60.

8. The presentation in this section draws heavily on Yoko Kitazawa, *From Tokyo to Johannesburg: A Study of Japan's Growing Economic Links with the Republic of South Africa* (New York: Interfaith Center for Corporate Responsibility, 1975).

9. *Ibid.*, p. 38.

10. *Africa Keizai Jijyo*, 20 July 1971; quoted in *ibid.*, p. 5.

11. *Star* (South Africa), 4 September 1971; quoted in Kitazawa, p. 11.

12. *Ibid.*, p. 10. In 1974 Japan announced that it would no longer grant deferred payment loans from the EXIM Bank to South Africa.

Chapter 4

1. The discussion of the early years of Japanese aid is taken from Alan G. Rix, *Japan's Economic Aid* (London: Croom Helm, 1980).

2. *Ibid.*, p. 223.

3. Alan G. Rix, "The Future of Japanese Foreign Aid," *Australian Outlook* 31, 3 (December 1977): 423.

4. John White, *Japanese Aid* (London: Overseas Development Institute 1964), p. 67; quoted in *ibid.*, p. 422.

5. For details, see Rix, *Japan's Economic Aid*, pp. 125-32.

6. *Ibid.*, pp. 223, 226.

7. JETRO, *Economic Cooperation of Japan 1980*, p. 19.

8. *Japan Times*, 29 September 1981.

Chapter 5

1. For details of the manner in which export credits were used to subsidize shipbuilding, see Chalmers Johnson, *MITI and the Japanese Miracle* (Stanford: Stanford University Press, 1982). p. 232.

2. Export-Import Bank of the United States, *Report to the U.S. Congress on Export Credit Competition and the Export-Import Bank of the United States for the Period January 1, 1981, through December 31, 1981* (Washington D.C., December 1982), p. 8.

3. *Ibid.*, pp. 20-24.

4. Richard E. Feinberg, *Subsidizing Success: The Export-Import Bank in the U.S. Economy* (Cambridge: Cambridge University Press, 1982), p. 80.

5. Export-Import Bank of the United States, *Report to the U.S. Congress*, pp. 65-66, 77.

6. OECD, DAC, *Investing in Developing Countries* (Paris, 1982), p. 112.

7. J.G. Gravelle and D.W. Kiefer, "Deferral and DISC: Two Targets of Tax Reform," in *Studies in Taxation, Public Finance and Related Subjects—A Compendium*, vol. 2 (Washington, D.C.: Fund for Public Policy Research, 1978).

8. Johnson, pp. 230-32.

9. Pauline H. Baker, "Obstacles to Private Sector Activities in Africa"; report prepared for U.S. Department of State, Bureau of Intelligence and Research, under contract no. 1722-220060, January 1983 (mimeo), pp. 70ff.

Chapter 6

1. Our findings that the success of Japanese corporations tends to be sectorally specific reinforce the conclusions reached by Ira C. Magaziner and Thomas M. Hout, *Japanese Industrial Policy* (Berkeley: Institute of International Studies, University of California, 1981); Policy Papers in International Affairs, no. 15.

2. Baker, ch. 5.

3. Lack of funding for the U.S. EXIM has been contrary to the recommendations made by Chester Crocker, Assistant Secretary of State for African Affairs, prior to his assumption of office. See, for instance, "African Policy in the 1980s," *Washington Quarterly* 3 (Summer 1980): 80.

4. For instance, see Lawrence B. Krause, *U.S. Economic Policy toward the Association of Southeast Asian Nations* (Washington, D.C.: Brookings Institution, 1982), pp. 82ff.

BIBLIOGRAPHY

Africa. No. 87 (November 1978): 109-24; no. 111 (November 1980): 59-74; no. 135 (November 1982): 84-92.

Agbi, Sunday O. *Japan's Attitudes and Policies Towards African Issues Since 1945: A Historical Perspective.* Tokyo: Institute of Developing Economies, 1982.

_____. "Africa—Japan's Continent-Sized Blind Spot." *Japan Times*, no.1 (June 1982).

Anderson, David. "America in Africa, 1981." *Foreign Affairs* 60, 3 (1982): 658-85.

Baker, Pauline. "Obstacles to Private Sector Activity in Africa." Report prepared for U.S. Department of State, Bureau of Intelligence and Research, under contract no. 1722-220060, January 1983. Mimeo.

Business Asia. 31 October 1980: 349-50.

Coker, Christopher. "Reagan and Africa." *World Today* 38, 4 (April 1982): 123-30.

Crocker, Chester A. "African Policy in the 1980s." *Washington Quarterly* 3, 3 (Summer 1980).

Feinberg, Richard E. *Subsidizing Success: The Export-Import Bank in the U.S. Economy.* Cambridge: Cambridge University Press, 1982.

Fujioka, Masao. *Japan's International Finance: Today and Tomorrow.* Tokyo: Japan Times, Ltd., 1979.

Fukai, Shigeko N. "Japan's North-South Dialogue at the United Nations." *World Politics* 35, 1 (October 1982): 73-105.

Fukunaga, Eiji. *Japan's Position Toward Africa: Documentary Compilation on Recent Moves.* Tokyo: Africa Society of Japan, 1975.

Gravelle, J. G., and Kiefer, D. W. "Deferral and DISC: Two Targets of Tax Reform." In *Studies in Taxation, Public Finance and Related Subjects—A Compendium*, vol. 2. Washington, D.C.: Fund for Public Policy Research, 1978.

Guide to the Africa Society of Japan. Tokyo: Africa Society of Japan, 1970.

Hasegawa, Sukehiro. *Japanese Foreign Aid: Policy and Practice.* New York: Praeger, 1975.

Hudson, Michael C. "Reagan's Policy in Northeast Africa." *Africa Report* 27, 2 (March/April 1982): 4-10.

Institute of Developing Economies. *Annual Report 1981-82.* Tokyo.

International Monetary Fund (IMF). *Direction of Trade Statistics Yearbook*, 1970-82.

Japan (Government of), Agency of Natural Resources and Energy and Ministry of International Trade and Industry. *Energy in Japan Facts and Figures.* July 1982.

_____, Economic Cooperation Bureau, Ministry of Foreign Affairs. *Japan's Economic Cooperation.* 1 July 1982.

_____, Export-Import Bank. *Annual Reports*, various years.

_____, Japanese National Committee of the World Petroleum Congress. *Petroleum Industry in Japan, 1981.* 1982.

_____, Japan External Trade Organization (JETRO). *Economic Cooperation of Japan, 1980.*

_____, _____. *Export Insurance System in Japan.* 1978.

_____, _____. *Japan Exports and Imports.* 1981.

_____, _____. *The Role of Trading Companies in International Commerce.* JETRO Marketing Series 2 (revised 1982).

_____, _____. *White Paper on International Trade*, 1971, 1973, 1976, 1982.

_____, Ministry of International Trade and Industry (MITI). *A Brief Introduction to Export Insurance Scheme of Japan.* 1981.

_____, _____. *Direct Overseas Investment from Japanese Companies*, various years.

_____, _____. "Direct Overseas Investment from Japanese Companies in Fiscal 1981." *News from MITI*, 23 June 1982.

_____, _____. "Economic Cooperation of Japan," 1980, 1981, 1982. Mimeo.

_____, _____. "Japan's Licensed Overseas Investments in Fiscal 1979." *News from MITI*, 14 July 1980.

_____, _____. "Japan's Licensed Overseas Investments in Fiscal 1980." *News from MITI*, 14 October 1981.

_____, _____. *Metal Mining Agency of Japan.* 1981.

_____, _____. *MITI Handbook.* June 1979.

_____, _____. "Outline of Existing Measures Concerning Direct Overseas Investment." August 1981.

_____, _____. *White Paper on International Trade, 1981.* 1981.

_____, _____. *White Paper on International Trade, 1982.* 1982.

_____, Sogo Shosha Committee of the Japan Foreign Trade Council. *The Sogo Shosha: What They Are and How They Can Work for You.* 1982.

"Japan and the Economic Development of the ASEAN Countries." *Export Industry Review* 1, 1 (1980): 32-46.

Bibliography

"Japanese Multinationals: Covering the World with Investment." *Business Week*, 16 June 1980: 92-99.

Japan Times (Tokyo). Various issues.

Johnson, Chalmers. *MITI and the Japanese Miracle: The Growth of Industrial Policy, 1925-1975*. Stanford: Stanford University Press, 1982.

Johnson, U. Alexis, and Packard, George R. *The Common Security Interests of Japan, the United States, and NATO*. Cambridge, Mass.: Ballinger, 1981.

Journal of Japanese Trade and Industry, no. 5 (1982): 20-22.

Kitazawa, Yoko. *From Tokyo to Johannesburg: A Study of Japan's Growing Economic Links with the Republic of South Africa*. New York: Interfaith Center for Corporate Responsibility, 1975.

Kojima, Kiyoshi. *Japan and a New World Economic Order*. Boulder, Colo.: Westview Press, 1977.

Krause, Lawrence B. *U.S. Economic Policy toward the Association of Southeast Asian Nations*. Washington, D.C.: Brookings Institution, 1982.

Magaziner, Ira C., and Hout, Thomas M. *Japanese Industrial Policy*. Berkeley: Institute of International Studies, 1981. Policy Papers in International Affairs, no. 15.

Masamichi, Chiyoura. "Investment Activities in Africa by Japanese Companies." *Economic Studies Institute Journal* (University of Dokyo, Soka, Japan), 1977.

Nakajima, Komei. "A Forecast on Trade Relations with African Nations." *Digest of Japanese Industry and Technology*, no. 175 (1982): 35-40.

Ogunremi, Gabriel O. *Nigeria-Japan Trade Relations, 1914-1979*. Tokyo: Institute of Developing Economies, 1980.

Organization for Economic Cooperation and Development (OECD), Development Assistance Committee (DAC). *Development Assistance*, various years.

_____, _____. *Development Cooperation*, various years.

_____, _____. *Flow of Financial Resources to Less Developed Countries*. Paris, 1964.

_____, _____. *Geographic Distribution of ODA Flows*. 1980.

_____, _____. *Investing in Developing Countries*. Paris, 1982.

Oriental Economist. October 1980: 38-43.

Overseas Uranium Resources Development Co., Ltd. *Outline of Overseas Uranium Resources Development Co., Ltd*. Tokyo, October 1982.

Ozawa, Terutomo. *Multinationalism, Japanese Style*. Princeton: Princeton University Press, 1979.

_____. "Japan's New Resource Diplomacy: Government-Backed Group Investment." *Journal of World Trade Law*, no. 14 (January/February 1980): 3-13.

Patrick, Hugh, and Rosovsky, Henry. *Asia's New Giant: How the Japanese Economy Works*. Washington, D.C.: Brookings Institution, 1976.

Radetzki, Marian. "Has Political Risk Scared Mineral Investment away from the Deposits in Developing Countries?" *World Development* 10, 1 (January 1982): 39-48.

Ravenhill, John. "Japan and Africa." In *Africa Contemporary Record, 1981-1982*, ed. Colin Legum. New York: Holmes and Meier, 1981, pp. A210-18.

Rix, Alan G. *Japan's Economic Aid*. New York: St. Martin's Press, and London: Croom-Helm, 1980.

_____. "The Future of Japanese Foreign Aid." *Australian Outlook* 31, 3 (December 1977): 418-38.

Rodrik, Dani, "Managing Resource Dependency: The United States and Japan in the Markets for Copper, Iron Ore and Bauxite." *World Development* 10, 7 (July 1982): 541-60.

Roth, Martin. "Japan and Africa." *Africa Economic Digest* 3, 49 (December 1982): 7-16.

Rothstein, Robert. *Global Bargaining*. Princeton: Princeton University Press, 1979.

United States (Government of), Department of Commerce. "Selected Data on U.S. Direct Investment Abroad," 1966-78.

_____, _____, Bureau of the Census. *U.S. Exports: World Trade by Commodity Groupings*, various years.

_____, _____, _____. *U.S. Imports: World Trade by Commodity Groupings*, various years.

_____, Department of State, Bureau of Public Affairs. *Africa: Economic Prospects and Problems*. Current Policy no. 422 (17 September 1982).

_____, Export-Import Bank. *Report to the U.S. Congress on Export Credit Competition and the Export-Import Bank of the United States for the Period January 1, 1981, through December 31, 1981*. Washington, D.C., December 1982.

_____, Office of Planning and Budgeting, Bureau for Program and Policy Coordination of the Agency for International Development. *U.S. Overseas Loans and Grants and Assistance from International Organizations: Obligations and Loan Authorizations*, 1 July 1945–30 September 1981.

_____, Trade Representative, Executive Office of the President. *Twenty-Fifth Annual Report of the President of the United States on the Trade Agreements Program 1980-1981*. 1982.

Vogel, Ezra F. "Guided Free Enterprise in Japan." *Harvard Business Review* 56, 3 (May/June 1978): 161-70.

West Africa, 22 November 1982: 3021-34.

Wheeler, Jimmy W., Janow, Merit E., and Pepper, Thomas. *Japanese Industrial Development Policies in the 1980s*. Croton-on-Hudson, N.Y.: Hudson Institute, 1982.

White, John. *Japanese Aid*. London: Overseas Development Institute, 1964.

Young, Alexander K. *The Sogo Shosha: Japan's Multinational Trading Companies*. Boulder, Colo.: Westview Press, 1979.

INDEX

145

Tanzania, 15, 18, 78, 82-83, 86, 87, 107, 113
Taxation, 105-6
Technical assistance, 65
Technology transfers, 63
Teikoku Oil company, 48
Telecommunications equipment, 34, 36, 111
Televisions, 34
Tessoum (Niger), 46
Textiles, 34, 40, 46, 111
Third World, 1-2, 66, 69, 82
Tobacco. *See* Food, beverages, and tobacco
Toyo Kogyo corporation, 62
Toyo Rubber corporation, 62
Toyota corporation, 62
Trading companies, 49, 58-60, 108, 114
Transportation equipment. *See* Machinery and transport equipment
Tropical products, 20

UDI. *See* Unilateral Declaration of Independence
Uganda, 15, 18, 78
UNCTAD. *See* United Nations Conference on Trade and Development
Unilateral Declaration of Independence (UDI), 5
United Kingdom, 4, 16, 99
United Nations, 64, 76
United Nations Conference on Trade and Development (UNCTAD), 66n

United States: anti-trust legislation of, 107-8, 116; diplomatic relations with Africa, 4-5, 112, 118; economic relations with Africa, 2, 6, 109; market shares in Africa, 19-22, 111; raw materials for, 2, 4; support for overseas activities, 88-89, 106, 108, 116; trade balance with Africa, 25, 27, 32-39, 110; trade by sectors, 111-12
Uranium, 27, 46, 64, 82, 91, 103, 113
USSR. *See* Soviet Union

White, John, 68
Wilcoxon-Mann-Whitney (W) test, 17
World Bank, 77
World Energy Development (Japan), 48

Yamaha corporation, 62
Yaoundé Conventions, 15
Yen, 41, 72, 73, 88
Yokohama Tire Company, 62

Zaire: aid to, 82, 83, 87; foreign government export promotions in, 100, 107; foreign market shares in, 19, 21-22, 48, 109; Japanese investments in, 43, 61, 113
Zambia, 19, 21-22, 43, 82, 86, 87, 91, 109
Zimbabwe, 87, 103, 107

JOANNA MOSS is Professor of Economics, San Francisco State University. She is the author of *The Lomé Conventions and Their Implications for the United States*.

JOHN RAVENHILL teaches international relations at the University of Sydney, Australia. He is the author of *Collective Clientelism: The Lomé Convention and North-South Relations*.

INSTITUTE OF INTERNATIONAL STUDIES
UNIVERSITY OF CALIFORNIA, BERKELEY

215 Moses Hall   Berkeley, California 94720

CARL G. ROSBERG, *Director*

Monographs published by the Institute include:

RESEARCH SERIES

1. *The Chinese Anarchist Movement.* R.A. Scalapino and G.T. Yu. ($1.00)
7. *Birth Rates in Latin America.* O. Andrew Collver. ($2.50)
15. *Central American Economic Integration.* Stuart I. Fagan. ($2.00)
16. *The International Imperatives of Technology.* Eugene B. Skolnikoff. ($2.95)
17. *Autonomy or Dependence in Regional Integration.* P.C. Schmitter. ($1.75)
19. *Entry of New Competitors in Yugoslav Market Socialism.* S.R. Sacks. ($2.50)
20. *Political Integration in French-Speaking Africa.* Abdul A. Jalloh. ($3.50)
21. *The Desert & the Sown: Nomads in Wider Society.* Ed. C. Nelson. ($5.50)
22. *U.S.-Japanese Competition in International Markets.* J.E. Roemer. ($3.95)
23. *Political Disaffection Among British University Students.* J. Citrin and D.J. Elkins. ($2.00)
24. *Urban Inequality and Housing Policy in Tanzania.* Richard E. Stren. ($2.95)
25. *The Obsolescence of Regional Integration Theory.* Ernst B. Haas. ($4.95)
26. *The Voluntary Service Agency in Israel.* Ralph M. Kramer. ($2.00)
27. *The SOCSIM Microsimulation Program.* E. A. Hammel et al. ($4.50)
28. *Authoritarian Politics in Communist Europe.* Ed. Andrew C. Janos. ($3.95)
29. *The Anglo-Icelandic Cod War of 1972-1973.* Jeffrey A. Hart. ($2.00)
30. *Plural Societies and New States.* Robert Jackson. ($2.00)
31. *Politics of Oil Pricing in the Middle East, 1970-75.* R.C. Weisberg. ($4.95)
32. *Agricultural Policy and Performance in Zambia.* Doris J. Dodge. ($4.95)
33. *Five Classy Computer Programs.* E.A. Hammel & R.Z. Deuel. ($3.75)
34. *Housing the Urban Poor in Africa.* Richard E. Stren. ($5.95)
35. *The Russian New Right: Right-Wing Ideologies in USSR.* A. Yanov. ($5.95)
36. *Social Change in Romania, 1860-1940.* Ed. Kenneth Jowitt. ($4.50)
37. *The Leninist Response to National Dependency.* Kenneth Jowitt. ($4.95)
38. *Socialism in Sub-Saharan Africa.* Eds. C. Rosberg & T. Callaghy. ($12.95)
39. *Tanzania's Ujamaa Villages: Rural Development Strategy.* D. McHenry. ($5.95)
40. *Who Gains from Deep Ocean Mining?* I.G. Bulkley. ($3.50)
41. *Industrialization & the Nation-State in Peru.* Frits Wils. ($5.95)
42. *Ideology, Public Opinion, & Welfare Policy: Taxes and Spending in Indusdustrialized Societies.* R.M. Coughlin. ($6.50)
43. *The Apartheid Regime: Political Power and Racial Domination.* Eds. R.M. Price and C. G. Rosberg. ($12.50)
44. *Yugoslav Economic System in the 1970s.* L.D. Tyson. ($5.50)
45. *Conflict in Chad.* Virginia Thompson & Richard Adloff. ($7.50)
46. *Conflict and Coexistence in Belgium.* Ed. Arend Lijphart. ($7.50)

47. *Changing Realities in Southern Africa.* Ed. Michael Clough. ($12.50)
48. *Nigerian Women Mobilized, 1900-1965.* Nina E. Mba. ($12.95)
49. *Institutions of Rural Development.* Eds. D. Leonard & D. Marshall. ($11.50)
50. *Politics of Women & Work in USSR & U.S.* J.C. Moses. ($9.50)
51. *Zionism and Territory.* Baruch Kimmerling. ($12.50)
52. *Soviet Subsidization of Trade with Eastern Europe.* M. Marrese & J. Vanous. ($14.50)
53. *Voluntary Efforts in Decentralized Management.* L. Ralston et al. ($9.00)
54. *Corporate State Ideologies.* C. Landauer. ($5.95)
55. *Effects of Economic Reform in Yugoslavia.* J. Burkett. ($9.50)
56. *The Drama of the Soviet 1960s.* A. Yanov. ($8.50)
57. *Revolutions and Rebellions in Afghanistan.* Eds. M.N. Shahrani & R.L. Canfield. ($14.95)
58. *Women Farmers of Malawi.* D. Hirschmann & M. Vaughan. ($8.95)

POLITICS OF MODERNIZATION SERIES

1. *Spanish Bureaucratic-Patrimonialism in America.* M. Sarfatti. ($2.00)
2. *Civil-Military Relations in Argentina, Chile, & Peru.* L. North. ($2.00)
9. *Modernization & Bureaucratic-Authoritarianism: Studies in South American Politics.* Guillermo O'Donnell. ($8.95)

POLICY PAPERS IN INTERNATIONAL AFFAIRS

1. *Images of Detente & the Soviet Political Order.* K. Jowitt. ($1.25)
2. *Detente After Brezhnev: Domestic Roots of Soviet Policy.* A. Yanov. ($4.50)
3. *Mature Neighbor Policy: A New Policy for Latin America.* A. Fishlow. ($3.95)
4. *Five Images of Soviet Future: Review & Synthesis.* G.W. Breslauer. ($4.50)
5. *Global Evangelism Rides Again: How to Protect Human Rights Without Really Trying.* E.B. Haas. ($2.95)
6. *Israel & Jordan: An Adversarial Partnership.* Ian Lustick. ($2.00)
7. *Political Syncretism in Italy.* Giuseppe Di Palma. ($3.95)
8. *U.S. Foreign Policy in Sub-Saharan Africa.* R.M. Price. ($4.50)
9. *East-West Technology Transfer in Perspective.* R.J. Carrick. ($5.50)
10. *NATO's Unremarked Demise.* Earl C. Ravenal. ($3.50)
11. *Toward Africanized Policy for Southern Africa.* R. Libby. ($7.50)
12. *Taiwan Relations Act & Defense of ROC.* E. Snyder et al. ($7.50)
13. *Cuba's Policy in Africa, 1959-1980.* William M. LeoGrande. ($4.50)
14. *Norway, NATO, & Forgotten Soviet Challenge.* K. Amundsen. ($3.95)
15. *Japanese Industrial Policy.* Ira Magaziner and Thomas Hout. ($6.50)
16. *Containment, Soviet Behavior, & Grand Strategy.* Robert Osgood. ($5.50)
17. *U.S.-Japanese Competition-Semiconductor Industry.* M. Borrus et al. ($7.50)
18. *Contemporary Islamic Movements in Perspective.* I. Lapidus. ($4.95)
19. *Atlantic Alliance, Nuclear Weapons, & European Attitudes.* W. Thies. ($4.50)
20. *War and Peace: The Views from Moscow and Beijing.* Banning N. Garrett & Bonnie S. Glaser. ($7.95)